The Tender Tyrant

THE TENDER TYRANT

Nadia Boulanger

A Life Devoted to Music

A Biography by
Alan Kendall

Introduction by Yehudi Menuhin

Lyceum Books
WILTON, CONNECTICUT

To my mother

First published in the United States in 1977 by
Lyceum Books, Inc., Wilton, Connecticut 06897
in cooperation with Macdonald and Jane's Publishers Limited,
Paulton House, 8 Shepherdess Walk, London N1

Copyright © Alan Kendall 1976

Edited by Felix Brenner

Library of Congress Catalog Card Number 76-27098.

Photoset and printed in Great Britain by
REDWOOD BURN LIMITED
Trowbridge & Esher

Contents

Author's Acknowledgments

I should like to thank the following for according me interviews or writing to me, often at length, and in some cases on more than one occasion:
Lennox Berkeley, Christopher Bochmann, Hugo Cole, Aaron Copland, Hugues Cuénod, Paul Derenne, David Diamond, Annette Dieudonné, Jay Gottlieb, Stephen Hicks, Winifred Hope Johnstone, Bernard Keeffe, Noël Lee, Raymond Leppard, Nicholas Maw, Jeremy Menuhin, Yehudi Menuhin, Zygmunt Mycielski, Mr and Mrs Alexander Tcherepnin, Virgil Thomson and Flore Wend.

I approached the following, and they very kindly indicated their willingness to collaborate, but for one reason or another – often the pressure of their work and of mine – I was unable to avail myself of their offer:
Leslie Bassett, Clifford Curzon, Thea Musgrave, Robin Orr, Walter Piston, Edwin Roxburgh, Louise Talma, David Ward and David Wilde.

I should also like to thank Linda Glick of the USIS library in London, Christopher Nowakowski of the Polish Cultural Institute in London, and the staff of the Windsor branch of the Berkshire County Library.

Last but by no means least, I should like to thank Brenda Holt for typing the manuscript so efficiently.

The quotations from Nadia Boulanger's own writings are translated by the author except where indicated.

The author and publishers wish to thank the following for permission to quote copyright material:

Marc Blancpain, of the Alliance Française; the estate of Eric Blom for quotations from *The Music Lover's Miscellany;* the British Broadcasting Corporation for quotations from their programme *The Tender Tyrant;* the editor of *Country Life* for extracts from Hugo Cole's article 'A Teacher of Infinite Humanity' (Vol. CLVI, No. 4019); Messrs J. M. Dent and Sons Ltd for an extract from Wilfrid Mellers' article 'Music and Society Now' in *Music and Western Man* (ed. Peter Garvie); Messrs Macdonald and Jane's for quotations from Aaron Copland's *Copland on Music;* The New York Times Company for quotations from Virgil Thomson's article on Nadia Boulanger of 4 February 1962; Messrs Peter Owen for a quotation from Gertrude Stein's *Paris France*, and Random House, Inc., for a quotation from Gertrude Stein's *The Autobiography of Alice B. Toklas.*

Attempts were made to contact all holders of copyright material, and failure to include acknowledgment here is no indication of intent to avoid such acknowledgment. Any omissions notified to the publishers will be included in future editions.

And the following for the use of illustrations:

1 to 7   courtesy Roger Violet, Paris
8   courtesy BBC, London

List of Illustrations

Preface

This book is intended essentially as a portrait of Nadia Boulanger and her world, and not as a biography. In the first place, as those who know anything about her at all will know full well, she shuns any glorification of herself, and indeed positively discourages it, preferring to conserve her energies for her work. When the idea of this book was first put to her, however, she did not refuse to have anything to do with it, as she might well have done, but always received me most cordially. On the other hand, she repeatedly made clear in her letters to me that in receiving me she was doing no more than she would for anyone else who wished to see her:

> 'Naturally I should be very pleased to see you, but I would not like you to have the impression that you will have the opportunity to "gossip" with me. I have so little free time. If you realize the situation, come and know that you will be *welcome*, but that the time devoted to these interviews will be of necessity short.'

In the event she was of great help, because she put me in touch with the people who would be likely to be of assistance, and because I had doubted all along whether I should ever get the sort of information from Nadia Boulanger herself that I would need to produce a true biography. That will have to come later.

A second, and much more compelling, reason why this is not a conventional biography, however, is that Nadia Boulanger's life has been her career. While one could list all the concerts she directed or performed in, and could attempt a compilation of a list of all the people who have studied with her, the result might be of restricted documentary interest, but would in no way begin to convey what the life of this extraordinary woman has meant to generations of people all over the world. I hope that in this book I have done something to convey her significance as a composer, pianist, conductor and music critic, but above all as a teacher of music.

Since the printed sources are very few indeed, I could not have done this without the help of many people in Europe and America, and I hope that the list printed in the author's acknowledgments is complete. I have tried to include everyone, and if anyone has been omitted, I sincerely apologize. There are, however, two people in particular that I must mention here. The first is Felix Brenner, who had the idea for the book in the first place, and had sufficient confidence in me to allow me to work unmolested over what turned out to be a rather longer period of time than we had anticipated. The second is Marcelle de Manziarly, who, after declaring that what I intended doing was 'hopeless', put her apartment and material at my disposal, and helped me in the most practical ways imaginable. To these two people, then, I owe the deepest gratitude, and can safely say that without them this book would never have been written.

Of course there will be some people who feel that they ought to have been consulted, and others who will possibly be offended at some of the things they find here. I have tried to treat everything I have read or been told as objectively as possible, but there were some things that I was unable to include. Their absence may make the picture slightly less complete, but in my view they in no way distort it.

On the other hand, this book is not intentionally eulogistic. I am well aware that there are people, whose judgement I must respect, who are critical of Nadia Boulanger. For my part I have never received anything but kindness and consideration from her, ever since I first went to her apartment in 1962, having graduated from Cambridge with little idea of what I was to do with myself. Although I was a total stranger, she gave me a long interview, listened to me carefully, and followed up the meeting with a very practical letter as to how I might pursue my career in Paris. Only years later did I realize that probably the most important factor of our first meeting was that she had taken me seriously.

Preface

If this book manages to portray a fraction of her achievement and significance, it will help to repay my private debt to her. My wish is that it may also act as a tribute from those of her friends who helped me with it, and that they will not be disappointed with the result. I hope Nadia Boulanger will not be displeased with it, either.

The Cloisters, Windsor Castle, January 1976

Introduction

In a world of such fluctuating and relative values, of such variety and confusion of standards of behaviour and of convictions, Nadia Boulanger is a fixed point – in itself an unbelievable achievement. But beyond this, she is a beacon and a guide-post for the many new generations which have flocked to her side during the course of her ninety years.

Children of all ages (for in her company we are all children, whether aged three or fifteen or thirty-five) of all types and nationalities, the brilliant and the less gifted, have found in her that for which they most dearly searched. They find a genuine love of the young, of the aspiring human animal, a very firm sense of direction and quality, great patience and perseverance which demand the very best that each can give, within his or her own limitations, and a personal self-discipline and dedication which never deny an obligation.

Temples, faiths, prejudices have all been submitted to critical and often withering analysis, and it is no wonder that our most firm convictions must now cling to relative quality, and no longer to dogma. Quality, spelled out, is tolerance combined with a ruthless dedication to the truths contained in the need to find logical forms, the need to expand our knowledge, and the constant search for beauty and love; it is openmindedness together with a supreme critical capacity for evaluation without condemning the unfit or the useless. Nadia Boulanger has been the cynosure for countless young musicians and has formed many of our foremost composers, each achieving a style utterly his or her own. This fixed point is quite literal, for Nadia Boulanger has occupied the same apartment for some seventy years.

She has never wavered in her singleminded dedication to her younger sister, and to her students; and Mademoiselle Boulanger, as she has always been known, leaves no-one in any doubt about her devout Catholicism, her unfailing respect for the hierarchy of worldly relationships. No-one in her presence could fail to respect the basic tenets of good behaviour and social graces, just as musically speaking they would not infringe on the basic disciplines which govern composition.

Nadia Boulanger has always insisted that music should be heard in the mind before it is committed to paper, and that every note in the score should have a meaningful function. Certainly there is no more acute ear in music that hers. Despite the discipline she evokes, she is anything but straightlaced. She accepted the dodecaphonic school and admired Stravinsky's and Berg's masterpieces without having to compromise her own norms, so broad and unprejudiced are these.

From the time of my own childhood in Paris I have admired and loved her, and now I have been privileged that her repeated visits have enabled the children of my School to share the same feelings I have. They almost feared her, but loved her more, and knew very well they had only their own lesser qualities to fear.

This book, which contains so much of her, happened characteristically without so much as an hour taken out of her daily routine. For this reason in its own way it conveys a reflection of the true Nadia Boulanger even more so than had the author enjoyed a series of personal interviews.

Yehudi Menuhin

1

The rue Ballu
and the Boulangers

The ninth *arrondissement* is hardly one the visitor to Paris is likely
to explore deliberately. It is essentially a district of offices,
banks and commercial undertakings, sandwiched between the
brighter attractions of Montmartre to the north and the Grands
Boulevards to the south, and between the more utilitarian
amenities of the Gare St-Lazare on the west and the Gare du
Nord on the east. The Opéra, it is true, stands at its south-west
corner, but the real ninth *arrondissement* lies behind that. The
church of the Trinité fills the vista at the end of the Chaussée
d'Antin, where Rossini ended his days in magnificent comfort,
and behind the Trinité, lodged between the rue de Clichy and
the rue Blanche as they climb up to Montmartre, lies a thin
wedge of Paris hardly large enough to be called a *quartier*; yet
here one suddenly leaves the twentieth century and plunges
into the calmer, more stately atmosphere of the nineteenth. The
streets are straight and the façades regular, proclaiming the
Paris of Napoléon III and Baron Haussmann. It is here in the
rue Ballu – named after the architect of the Trinité, who died
only two years before she was born – that for more than half a
century Nadia Juliette Boulanger has received generations of
musicians from all over the world.

It is fitting that she should have remained in this corner of
Paris and never moved to a more fashionable quarter or a more
opulent apartment. It would be difficult to imagine her anywhere else. For musicians (most of them from abroad, because
relatively few of the French have felt the call), this place has
become a shrine. In fact, the 'standing' of the rue Ballu might
almost be taken as an indication of Nadia Boulanger's stature

in France. It is quintessentially French, and therefore taken for granted by the French, so that only foreigners would find anything remarkable or unusual in it. Those who find this point of view too naive have been heard to accuse other French musicians and teachers of jealousy. Be that as it may, it is hard for the uninitiated from abroad to understand this apparent lack of recognition. A new pupil, making his first visit to the apartment, inadvertently entered the wrong staircase and so rang the wrong doorbell. A distinguished looking old gentleman opened the door.

'*S'il vous plaît, monsieur, Mademoiselle Boulanger.*'

'*Boulanger, boulanger? Il n'y a pas de boulanger ici.*'

'There's no baker here . . .' If he was aware that someone called Boulanger lived nearby, the fact remained that the name Nadia Boulanger meant nothing to him; yet it is well known to people from all over the world.

There is little to indicate the presence of such a distinguished inhabitant at 36 rue Ballu. The elevator looks as if it has been there since elevators were invented. Its flowery wrought-ironwork seems so insubstantial, its movement so sedate and its capacity so minute, that most visitors capable of walking up the red-carpeted staircase tend to do so.

Again, the entrance to the apartment reveals nothing unusual in its bare parquet floors and matt surface walls. (The French for some reason have never been introduced to the benefits of gloss paint.) There do, however, seem to be a surprisingly large number of hooks on the coat rack, and the 'overflow', one discovers, extends through the service door into the corridor beyond; but this is the only hint of the numbers that habitually arrive for Wednesday afternoons.

From the entrance hall one moves into what is most frequently used as a waiting room. It has recently been painted in a rich yellow, almost the colour of butter, and this background shows off to admirable effect the portrait of Nadia's father, with his dark hair and penetrating gaze. One contemplates the plaster cornice, the French windows and the double doors, the marble fireplace and the looking glass over it (which fills the whole of the chimney breast up to the ceiling), and one realizes that this house dates from the last time urban building took place on a grand scale, with a confident belief in what was necessary for the pursuit of a family's life from day to day.

From the murmur of voices beyond the half-open double doors one senses that the sanctum is within. It is more than twice the size of the outer room, with two French windows giving on to a balcony, and much of the wall facing them taken up with glass doors leading into the dining room. Since these are open most of the time, the impression of space is increased, and yet one is aware that this floor was certainly not the *piano nobile* of the house, for the ceiling is in fact quite low.

The far end of the room as one enters it is almost completely filled with a chamber organ. To the left, filling the space between the windows, is one grand piano, and to the right, filling the wall between the doorway and the dining room doors, is the second grand piano. Immediately on the left stands the inevitable marble fireplace, with its looking glass. There may often be a vase of beautiful flowers, and yet the whole effect of this room is one of soft, muted colours. The light is filtered through net curtains, and the walls are a soft pearly grey. Nothing jars, nothing stands out, and it takes a while for the eyes to adjust to this new tonality, and begin to notice the details.

The 'second' piano is covered with a faded cloth, on which stand numerous signed photographs; over the fireplace is a white marble bust of Lili, Nadia Boulanger's younger sister, again standing on a faded, perhaps once sumptuous, piece of fabric. Then there is the chair at the keyboard, where countless notes have been played and opinions pronounced. Behind it is an alcove with shelves, but the eye cannot make out the contents, and one would not venture to peer. Besides, that is not why one is there.

The character of the room is neither ostentatious nor shabby. Occasionally a jarring note is introduced when a record player is rigged up for Wednesday afternoons, and trailing speaker wires and bright veneers look out of place; but when it has been removed, the traditional calm is restored, and conversation may resume. This, then, is the room that generations of people, some famous and many totally forgotten or unknown, of widely varying talents but including some of the most consummate musicians of this century, have come to know and associate for ever with Nadia Boulanger.

Nadia Boulanger's paternal grandfather Frederick was a 'cello teacher attached to the Chapel Royal, and he married a singer, Marie-Julie Halligner, who was born in Paris on 29 January 1786. She entered the Conservatoire (which had been founded in 1795), to study *solfeggio* on 20 March 1806, and took singing lessons from Plantade. Then in January 1807 she became a pupil of Garat, who had sung before Marie-Antoinette at Versailles in January 1783. Marie-Julie had a very beautiful voice, and her vocal technique was brilliant and supple. Whenever she sang at concerts, she had a great success.

On 16 March 1811 she made her début at the Opéra-Comique in *L'ami de maison* and *Le concert interrompu*. Her success was overwhelming, and at the end she was brought back on to the stage to the cheers of a delighted audience. In fact she became such a box-office draw that the management of the theatre prolonged her début for a whole year. She obviously had great talent for acting, particularly for comedy, which, allied to her beautiful voice, made her much sought after. At this time, when the advent of grand opera, and the Italian tradition in particular, had made weighty singers – despite dramatic requirements – all too common on the stage, Marie-Julie must indeed have been worth going to see and hear. We are only now seeing truly graceful heroines who look as if they might genuinely be dying of consumption, and tenors who look as if they could inspire affection in their hearts.

Marie-Julie was described as having 'a happy mixture of gaiety, sensitivity and finesse', which might almost be a description of her grand-daughter Nadia, whom she unfortunately never met. Her career continued successfully for some eighteen years or so, and then something disastrous happened to her voice, forcing her to retire in April 1845 with a pension from the Opéra-Comique. A ruptured aneurysm – the morbid dilation of an artery – killed her on 23 July 1850, at the age of sixty-four.

Marie-Julie's son, Nadia's father, was born in Paris on 16 September 1815. He was christened Ernest Henri Alexandre, and entered the Conservatoire on 18 January 1830, where he studied *solfeggio* with Valentin Alkan, and counterpoint with Halévy. When one recalls that Alkan was a friend of Chopin and Liszt, and that Halévy numbered among his pupils

Gounod and Bizet, one begins to understand how the Boulanger family came to be steeped in music. Ernest also studied
with Lesueur for 'dramatic style'.

Lesueur was an extraordinary character, who weathered all
the storms from the Revolution to the Restoration, and wrote
reams of operas, masses and oratorios, whose characteristics
Berlioz described as being most remarkable for 'the strangeness
of the melodies, their antique tonal colours and their dreamy
harmonies'. Lesueur was one of the founders of Romantic
Opera, and must have influenced the young Ernest.

In 1835 Ernest Boulanger won first prize for composition in
the Grand Prix de Rome, a competition organized by the Institute of France, with his cantata *Achille*. In the December of that
year he set off for Italy with a government scholarship, thus
starting a family tradition in the Prix de Rome that both his
daughters were to follow.

The Academy of Fine Arts of the Institute of France awards
each year, and has done so since 1803, scholarships that entitle
the winners to live in Rome for four years at the Villa Medici.
This marvellous opportunity for uninterrupted work, free from
the worries of finding board and lodging, is basically a splendid
and practical one, but unfortunately it has always been the
centre of a great deal of controversy. Some of this would have
been almost inevitable, since competitions in the field of the arts
are almost impossible to run in any satisfactory way, and the
Prix de Rome is awarded for painting, sculpture, engraving,
architecture and music. In music the competition is based on
the writing of a cantata on a given subject, and while they are
writing, the candidates are locked in a room for a number of
days. There have to be preliminary tests, to make sure that all
the candidates are of reasonable calibre, and obviously, for a
gifted and enthusiastic young composer, this process might
very well be odious. Berlioz made no less than five attempts at
it, and was moved to write about it to Humbert Ferrand in the
following terms in 1827:

'Must I demean myself so far as to compete once more? I must, for
my father wishes it and attaches much importance to the prize. For
his sake I will be represented and will write them a homely composition which will be quite as effective when played on the piano as

by the richest orchestra; I will be lavish in redundancies, because they are the forms to which the great masters adhered, and one must not do better than the great masters. And if I gain the prize, I will swear to you that I will tear up my *Scène* before the very eyes of these gentlemen as soon as the prize has been awarded to me.' (*Les Musiciens et la musique*)

In the event, despite a hopeless love for the Irish actress Harriet Smithson and the Revolution of 1830, he won the Grand Prix easily with his *Sardanapale* in July of that year. This was also the year in which he wrote the *Symphonie fantastique*, finished on 5 December, a few days before his twenty-seventh birthday.

Debussy was another great French composer who tried more than once for the Prix de Rome, winning it at the second attempt in 1884 with his cantata *L'enfant prodigue*. His time in Rome was not particularly productive, however, and Liszt advised him to listen to the music of Lassus and Palestrina in an attempt to remedy the situation. Debussy also heard Wagner's *Lohengrin*, and later went to Bayreuth twice, in 1888 and 1889, but much of what he wrote at the Villa Medici was either destroyed, lost or left unfinished. There was his setting of Théodore de Banville's *Diane au bois*, which he put aside in order to enter for the Prix de Rome and never took up again; there was *Printemps* for orchestra, which may have been written in 1887, but which he completely re-orchestrated and published in 1908; and there was his *Fantaisie*, for piano and orchestra, which was only published posthumously in 1919 – but these are only a part of the output of this period of his career.

Among the writings published under the title of *Monsieur Croche, antidilettante*, Debussy gave his opinion about the Prix de Rome:

> '"Among the institutions on which France prides herself, do you know any more ridiculous than the institution of the Prix de Rome? I am aware that this has often been said and still more often written, but apparently without any effect, since it continues to exist with that deplorable obstinacy which distinguishes absurd ideas."
>
> 'I ventured to answer that possibly the institution derived its strength from the fact that it had attained in certain circles to the position of a superstition. To have won or not to have won the Prix de Rome settled the question of whether one did or did not possess talent. If it was not absolutely certain, it was at least convenient and

provided public opinion with a sort of ready-reckoner.'

Possibly the most notorious case was that of Ravel, who competed regularly. At the age of twenty-six he won the second prize, which Nadia Boulanger had also won, but that does not carry with it residence in Rome. Two years later there were strong protests when he failed again, and his teacher Fauré entered the fray. At the age of thirty, when he already had such compositions as *Pavane pour une infante défunte, Jeux d'eau* and the string quartet behind him, the authorities would not even let him sit for the competition on the grounds that the preliminary tests were not satisfactory. In the ensuing scandal, and after a vigorous newspaper campaign, Dubois, the Director of the Conservatoire, resigned, and Fauré was elected in his place in 1905.

Ernest Boulanger caused no such scandal. He came back to Paris towards the end of 1839, and began to look for a poem that he could use as the libretto for an opera. He eventually found one from the hand of Scribe, who gave him the scraps left over from *Robert le Diable*, which Meyerbeer had composed in 1831. Ernest Boulanger's one-act opera was entitled *Le diable à l'école*, and had its première in January 1842. The work was well received, and fulfilled some of his earlier promise. In the following January the appearance of a second opera, *Les deux bergères*, confirmed his status as an operatic composer in the lighter vein. Two more one-act operas – *Une voix* and *Les sabots de la marquise* – were staged in 1845, and in August 1847 a three-act work entitled *La cachette* was performed.

After this the works appeared less regularly – in the words of one biographer, 'he seemed to have despaired of himself'. *Don Quichotte*, an opera in three acts, was performed at the Théâtre Lyrique in 1869, and *Don Mucarade*, in one act, at the Opéra-Comique in May 1875. There were also some operettas, such as *La meunière de Sans Souci* and *Marion*, which were published but never performed. In 1871, however, Ernest Boulanger had been made a singing teacher at the Conservatoire, having received the Legion of Honour in August 1869.

The family lived, therefore, in a world of music, though the young Nadia did not approve of it all. Fauré was a friend of the family, but so was Ambroise Thomas, and it is fair to say that

Ernest Boulanger's music had more in common with the latter's than the former's. As a benign father he accepted his daughter's criticisms, but ventured to suggest that one day she would modify her opinion – which she did. He survived to see in the new century, and died on 14 April 1900.

Nadia's mother Raïssa, the Russian Princess Michetsky, was born in St Petersburg in 1858. She studied singing with Ernest, and despite the fact that he was some forty-three years her senior, she married him when she was nineteen in 1877, and gave birth to their first daughter, Juliette, on 16 January 1885. Juliette died on 16 April of the following year, but happily there were another two daughters – Nadia Juliette, born on 16 September 1887; and Lili Juliette Marie Olga, born on 21 August 1893, whom Nadia always referred to as *La Petite*. Bearing in mind the fact that Madame Boulanger lived until 1935, it is amazing to realize that her life, together with that of her husband, spanned a period of 120 years. With no academic grounding, Nadia's mother took it upon herself to learn harmony so that she could teach her daughters the rudiments of music. In this way Nadia was able to read music fluently by the age of five, and her mother was always an important influence in her life.

Lili's health prevented her from following any regular course of study before the age of sixteen, and it was to her elder sister, after her mother, that she owed most of her initial musical education. When the family settled in 36 rue Ballu in 1904, Nadia, at the age of seventeen, first began to teach privately and, of course, Lili became her most important pupil. Lili entered the Conservatoire in 1909, and studied composition with Georges Caussade and Paul Vidal. Stylistic comparisons are notoriously unhelpful, even positively misleading on occasion, but if Lili Boulanger had affinities with any composers, one might point to Mussorgsky, Debussy, and, naturally, Fauré, with whom she and her sister studied. However, as Marcelle de Manziarly has pointed out, she found her own musical personality almost at once, 'with the instinct of a genius marked by death'.

In 1913 Lili Boulanger was the first woman to receive the premier Grand Prix de Rome for music, with her cantata *Faust et Hélène*. For her sister she was, in Nadia's own words, a guide and example. It is difficult to see exactly how she might have developed, and yet many people agree that she displayed immense promise, and might have become a great composer, had she lived. What we have is certainly extremely talented for one so young.

A list of the principal works that survive is useful, but does not reveal a great deal: *Nocturne* (for flute or violin and piano), 1911; *Pour les funérailles d'un soldat* (orchestra), 1912; *Clairières dans le ciel* (tenor and piano) to poems of F. Jammes, 1914; *Faust et Hélène* (cantata), 1913, which she conducted in performance in 1915; *Three psalms* (soloists, choir and orchestra), 1916–17; *Vieille prière bouddhique* (choir and orchestra), 1917; *La Princesse Malène* (unfinished opera) to text of Maeterlinck; and *Pie Jésus* (soprano, strings, harp and organ), her last work, 1918. She died of tuberculosis that year on 15 March.

It was the experience of teaching Lili that made Nadia decide to leave composing to others. She made up her mind to devote herself to encouraging, guiding and developing her sister's talent, because she felt that her own gifts as a composer were inferior by far to those of her sister. She has of course written pieces, some of which are published, and is reported to have said that if she were to relive her time she would not give up composing so soon – not because she feels she would have produced any great work, but because she feels it is good for a musician to practise composition.

What this devotion to Lili's talent did do, however, was to reveal to Nadia her own ability as a teacher, and ultimately to the world that she was a teacher of the first order, and a very rare phenomenon. As the Swiss tenor Hugues Cuénod has said: 'Her teaching has influenced generations of composers and generations of musicians who, in their turn, influenced others, and I think that, in a way, it is something like musical christianity, you know.'

It was an interesting simile, for on a completely different occasion Yehudi Menuhin said that it was as if Nadia Boulanger had founded her own religious order, with herself as the sole member. As an afterthought he said that he could not possibly imagine that she could ever have to confess. Certainly her devotion has a religious quality, but this should not blind us to her capacity for intense emotion and an ability to feel that amounts to passion. As one of her more recent students, the Englishman Stephen Hicks, has said: 'The thing is that she related everything to life because I think she herself led a very passionate inner life'; and according to Henryk Szeryng, the distinguished violinist, 'There was always an excitement to everything she taught, to everything she explained'.

When asked in 1973 what advice she would give to a young musician, she replied: 'Do not take up music unless you would rather die than not do so. It must be an indissoluble love. And one with the great joy of learning, the firm determination to learn, the unswerving perseverance, the intense faithfulness. But primarily if it is *not* better to die than not do music – then it is an excuse. And if not, then why, why?'

Her great determination and dedication, indeed her single-mindedness of purpose, which have given some of her pupils wonderful support and yet crushed others at times, carried her through the personal tragedies and setbacks in her own life. Nadia's very weak vision, for example, which has so troubled her in her latter years and which she has so remarkably overcome in her eighties, was manifest at a very early age. In fact the doctors said that it would be unwise for her to read both music and French together, and that a choice would have to be made. Happily music was the winner.

She won first prize at the Conservatoire for harmony in 1903, and carried off the prizes for organ, piano accompaniment and fugue in 1904. She was awarded the Second Grand Prix de Rome for composition with her cantata *La sirène* in 1908, and in the following year began teaching at the Conservatoire as an *assistante* to Dallier in harmony.

When asked whether she had written any music of her own, she replied '*Hélas, oui*', and went on to describe it as '*musique . . . pas mauvaise, mais inutile*'. And in a way she is quite right. The twelve songs, for example, published by Hamelle in 1909 are pleasant, but very reminiscent of Fauré. On the cover of the first one her name managed to be misspelt as Boulenger, but was subsequently corrected. In addition there is a *Rhapsodie* for piano and orchestra, her cantata *La sirène* and some organ music. There are also some songs published by Heugel, *Les heures claires*, to texts by the Belgian poet Emile Verhaeren (1855–1916), written in collaboration with Raoul Pugno, as well as an unpublished work, inspired by D'Annunzio, called *La ville morte*.

Pugno, who was born in the Parisian suburb of Montrouge on 23 June 1852, was a pupil at the Ecole Niedermeyer and at the Conservatoire, where he won first prizes for piano in 1866, harmony in 1867 and organ in 1869. For twenty years, from 1872 to 1892, he was choirmaster at the church of St Eugène. Then he went back to the Conservatoire to teach harmony until 1896 and piano from 1896 to 1901. He wrote music for piano, ballets, operettas and light operas, and even an oratorio, as well as publishing a book of lessons and a book on Chopin, but his chief fame rests on his career as a virtuoso pianist, and the recitals that he gave with the violinist Ysaye. One of their most frequently performed items was the César Franck sonata for violin and piano, which was dedicated to Ysaye; but they did much to popularize a much wider repertoire, especially works by Saint-Saëns, Vincent d'Indy, Fauré and Chausson.

In his *Monsieur Croche, antidilettante* Debussy made a reference to Pugno as a virtuoso, along with Ysaye, which at first glance may be taken as condemning the artistes themselves but in fact is really aimed at the French public and its love of virtuosity for its own sake:

'The attraction of the virtuoso for the public is very like that of the circus for the crowd. There is always the hope that something dangerous may happen: M. Ysaye may play the violin with M. Colonne on his shoulders; or M. Pugno may conclude his piece by lifting the piano with his teeth.'

Pugno obviously found a kindred spirit in Nadia Boulanger. She always remembered certain of his interpretations long after he was dead, in particular that of the César Franck *Symphonic Variations*. She regarded his conception of it as 'architectural', and the most authentic there was likely to be of the work. Performances of it, even thirty or more years after his death, automatically made her think of him.

Late in the year 1913 Nadia accompanied Raoul Pugno on a tour of Russia. It was fascinating for her to see the country of her mother's birth, from which one of the most important influences in her life – that of Igor Stravinsky – was to come. Many Western artistes had been attracted to Russia for some time.

These performers were received by their Russian hosts with an extravagant display of luxurious accommodation and appreciation of their talents. Every attention was lavished upon them, though in a style strongly contrasting with what they were accustomed to in their native lands. The actress Françoise Rosay made the long journey from France to play a season in St Petersburg (she sang in opera in those days), and the 'cellist Pablo Casals went from Spain to give recitals. He was astonished to find that he was expected to walk over the backs of prostrate servants as he left the room after a performance. But Nadia's fascinating and exciting tour came to an abrupt and tragic end when Pugno died suddenly in Moscow at the age of sixty-one on 3 January 1914. Nine months later the holocaust erupted and a world war and revolution completely destroyed that former existence.

After the unprecedented slaughter, the end of World War One brought relief to many, but little personal solace to Nadia Boulanger. Pugno had died, as well as her beloved Lili early in 1918, so that her mother was the only family left to her. The loss of her younger sister profoundly marked her life, and the anniversary of her sister's death, 15 March, is to this day one of deep grief. Many people, while admiring her devotion to the cause of her sister's music, deplore her annual observance of her death and that of their mother, as well as the perpetual mourning Nadia wears. But although death saddens Nadia Boulanger, as a Christian, and a Roman Catholic in particular, she is a fervent believer in the life hereafter. Indeed, when preparing the sleeve notes for the record of Lili's *Pie Jésus* (assisted by the American David Noakes), Nadia wrote:

'Such music lies beyond the reach of commentary; but there seems to be a natural affinity between the feeling of ineffable serenity conveyed by the composer at this ultimate hour and such an evocation as John Donne's when he speaks of "where we shall end, and yet begin but then; where we shall have continuall rest, and yet never grow lazie; where we shall be stronger to resist, and yet have no enemy; where we shall live and never die, where we shall meet and never part".'

This last, for Nadia Boulanger, is the bedrock of her belief.

From that time her pupils were to become her family. Her life was to be devoted to music and musicians, and with her musical background everything was in Nadia's favour, except perhaps her sex. Few women had ever had the temerity to strike out on their own in the world of music, a world almost totally dominated by men. It has never appeared to bother Nadia Boulanger, though at times it has seemed to bother some of those who have come into contact with her.

In 1920 she became a professor at the École Normale de Musique, teaching harmony, counterpoint, accompaniment and the history of music. (She was to remain there until 1939, taking over the composition class from Dukas on his death in 1935.) The next year, 1921, was the year in which the American Conservatory was created at Fontainebleau, and so it was the *annus mirabilis*, the year in which Nadia Boulanger's career took on a truly new dimension. Three Americans, Aaron Copland, Melville Smith and Virgil Thomson, then found her more or less independently, and a small trickle of foreign students soon grew to a flood. It is interesting to consider what sort of person she was in those days. Virgil Thomson, in his autobiography, described her in this way:

'Nadia Boulanger, then thirty-four, taught harmony at the Conservatoire, organ-playing and counterpoint at the École Normale de Musique. A tall, soft-haired brunette still luscious to the eye, she had already resigned womanly fulfillment and vowed her life to the memory of her sister . . . to the care of her long-widowed mother (who had married her elderly voice teacher at eighteen), and to musically bringing up the young. A certain maternal warmth was part of her charm for all young men; but what endeared her most to Americans was her conviction that American music was about to "take off" just as Russian music had done eighty years before.

'. . . I didn't go to France to study with Nadia Boulanger, I went to France to study. I had no idea who Nadia Boulanger was. I had a fellowship from Harvard University, for spending a year or so abroad. And there were two of those fellowships. The man who had had the one the previous year was in Paris when I arrived, and I said "Who've you been studying with?" He told me of his adventures in finding teachers, and he'd come upon Nadia Boulanger only that spring. Aaron Copland discovered her the same summer by going to the American Conservatory in Fontainebleau, which had just opened at that time.'

Or again, Aaron Copland writing of her tells how she emitted

'. . . a kind of objective warmth. She had none of the ascetic intensity of a Martha Graham nor the toughness of a Gertrude Stein. On the contrary, in those early days she possessed an almost old-fashioned womanliness – a womanliness that seemed quite unaware of its own charm. Her low-heeled shoes and long black skirts and pince-nez glasses contrasted strangely with her bright intelligence and lively temperament.'

The first wave of American pupils included – in addition to Aaron Copland, Virgil Thomson and Melville Smith – Elliott Carter, Theodore Charles, Herbert Elwell, Roy Harris, Douglas Moore, Walter Piston and Roger Sessions. Of all of this group, the first two have probably done most to bring to the world's attention, through their writings, what in their opinion are the most important aspects of Nadia Boulanger's career.

Aaron Copland was born in Brooklyn in 1900. At seventeen he began harmony lessons with Rubin Goldmark, and then at the age of twenty-one he went to Paris to study, first with Paul Vidal. It was through a chance introduction that he encountered Nadia Boulanger, who was not known in America at the time. Copland wanted to see what was going on in France from a musical point of view, and he found Nadia Boulanger through a harpist called Djina Ostrowska, who was at the newly created American Conservatory. He admits that the fact she was a woman constituted something of a hurdle to him at first, but nevertheless he became one of the first Americans to study with her. As he wrote in *Copland on Music*:

'Curiously enough I have no memory of discussing the role of women in music with Mademoiselle. Whatever her attitude may have been, she herself was clearly a phenomenon for which there was no precedent. In my own mind she was a continuing link in that long tradition of the French intellectual woman in whose salon philosophy was expounded and political history made. In similar fashion Nadia Boulanger had her own salon where musical aesthetics were argued and the musical future engendered.'

Among the great people whom Aaron Copland met there, or at least rubbed shoulders with, were Maurice Ravel, Igor Stravinsky, Albert Roussel, Darius Milhaud, Arthur Honegger, Francis Poulenc and Georges Auric in the musical world, and

Paul Valéry and Paul Claudel in the literary world. The latest works of Thomas Mann, Gide and Proust were discussed, as were the recent developments in almost all branches of the arts, so that the world of the rue Ballu was a marvellous stimulus not only to the musical education of the young Americans, but also their basic culture.

Paris was the catalyst in this way and at this time through a curious mixture of tradition, history and accident. It is a recurring theme – in fact almost the main theme – of Gertrude Stein's *Paris France*, written at the beginning of World War Two, which gave the author a point from which to survey the century until then. She never lived to see what it was like after that upheaval, and although in some respects Paris continued to be what it had always been for some on the surface, in fact times had changed, and were never to be the same again. This gives her book all the more significance, because she had been there – an integral part of it, if not one of its creators. She saw clearly what Paris had to offer people like Aaron Copland, and many more who flocked there:

'. . . what made Paris and France the natural background of the art and literature of the twentieth century. Their tradition kept them from changing and yet they naturally saw things as they were, and accepted life as it is, and mixed things up without any reason at the same time. Foreigners were not romantic to them, they were just facts, nothing was sentimental they were just there, and strangely enough it did not make them make the art and literature of the twentieth century but it made them be the inevitable background for it.'

This last point is important, because it shows that even in those days Gertrude Stein at least knew it was not the French who were blazing the trail for twentieth-century art and literature – a fact that became even more apparent in the years after the war than it did at the time she was writing. Paris was simply the setting, the stage upon which the artistic young made their débuts. The French may be forgiven for imagining that they were the motive force, when in fact they were merely providing the location. To a culturally young country such as America at this time, however, the provision of such a background was of vital importance; and one must not underestimate the nature of the setting – centuries of refinement and tradition, which had made Paris a burning focus of artistic energy.

It was as if all that Western Europe had to offer was concentrated there at that epoch. When Aaron Copland discovered Nadia Boulanger, it certainly seemed that way to him: 'Nadia Boulanger knew everything there was to know about music; she knew the oldest and the latest music, pre-Bach and post-Stravinsky, and knew it cold.' It was as if he had been given a key to the store of musical knowledge.

When he returned home from France, he took charge of the League of Composers, taught at the New School for Social Research from 1927 to 1937, and cemented a relationship with the Boston Symphony Orchestra that had begun when Walter Damrosch conducted his Symphony for Organ and Orchestra with Nadia Boulanger as soloist in 1925. From then on a succession of new works that Copland produced each year for the next five or six years were given their first performances by the Boston Symphony, under its regular conductor, Serge Koussevitsky. Copland also wrote magazine articles and did an immense amount to make America aware of its new composers.

From 1928 to 1931 Copland shared with Roger Sessions the Copland-Sessions concerts, at which both American and European works were played, and he continued this kind of association with Roy Harris when he returned from studying with Nadia Boulanger in 1931, and then with Walter Piston in 1935. In that year Copland took Piston's composition class at Harvard. In 1937 Copland, Virgil Thomson and Marc Blitzstein – all Boulanger pupils – together with Lehman Engel, founded the Arrow Music Press and the American Composers' Alliance.

The breadth and scope of Copland's activity gives some indication of what is probably his most notable quality as a composer over and above the music itself, and that is his professionalism. He decided what he felt needed doing, and set out to do it. In particular he tried to reach a public that had been brought up with the radio, gramophone and cinema. 'It made no sense', he wrote, 'to ignore the new public and to write as if they did not exist. I felt that it was worth the effort to see if I couldn't say what I had to say in the simplest possible terms.'

From this point of view there is a marked similarity between the declared intents of Copland and those of Benjamin Britten in England, and it is not surprising to learn that the two men are friends. Copland contributed an essay to the volume published to celebrate Britten's fiftieth birthday in 1963. Virgil Thomson, writing about Copland, stresses another point of similarity between Britten and Copland – of their concern to be of service to the public at large:

> 'He yearned for a large public; the social-service ideals of the 1930s and the musical successes of Dmitri Shostakovich having created in him a strong desire to break away from the over-intellectualized and constricting modernism of his Paris training. Stravinsky's neo-classical turn toward conservatism, initiated in 1918, had offered guidance to the postwar School of Paris and to all those still-young Americans, by the 1930s quite numerous and influential, who through Nadia Boulanger had come under its power.'

But as Thomson went on to point out, they had all put up a façade of dissonance, which was making for monotony and inflexibility, especially when applied to every sort of music; this was a particular problem in the theatre, where ballet, opera and incidental music were affected. One way out was an exploration of jazz idiom, which did not work for Copland, and the other was an exploration of America's folk music, which did. Of course to say as much is to indulge in dangerous over-simplification, and ignores Copland's serial music totally, but his most widely known and most popular works tend to be those that are most appreciably American in flavour.

Virgil Thomson – along with Copland and Melville Smith – was the third member of that first trio of Americans to study with Nadia Boulanger. His own opinion is that if he is to be remembered by any of his music it will be for his operas, two of which – *Four Saints in Three Acts* and *The Mother of Us All* – are to texts by Gertrude Stein. Be that as it may, we are extremely lucky that he is so articulate, and has committed his recollections, criticisms and predictions to paper, with a touch of slightly wry humour on occasions.

Not all composers are articulate, and even if they are, many prefer to use their time and mental energy for composing. It is good that some are capable of communicating in this way, however, to the non-musical members of the community. Aaron Copland, in writing about the difficult path of development from student exercises to mature composing, wonders how the teacher's knowledge can be passed on in a creative art at all:

> 'And yet it happens: some kind of magic does indubitably rub off on the pupil. It begins, perhaps, with the conviction that one is in the presence of an exceptional musical mentality [i.e. Nadia Boulanger]. By a process of osmosis one soaks up attitudes, principles, reflections, knowledge. That last is a key word: it is literally exhilarating to be with a teacher for whom the art one loves has no secrets.'

Virgil Thomson, however, puts his finger exactly on what makes Nadia Boulanger special:

> '. . . her real power as a teacher came from her extraordinarily acute critical sense. I had never previously had a teacher, nor have I encountered very many since around the world, who knew so instantly what one's music was about. Each piece of it that one showed to her, she seemed to understand and not reproach one with.'

Reproach must surely, for the aspiring composer, or indeed for any student in the creative arts, be the hardest thing to bear. Thomson continued:

> 'My previous instructors had usually managed to create the impression that composing music was a risky procedure because you were really in competition with Beethoven and Brahms, and you'd better look out. Well she had no such attitude. For her, writing music was like writing a letter, it's a function of the musical mind, and in that way she put me at my ease in front of the music paper, so that I wasn't writing Beethoven's music, I was writing my own, and my own was perfectly modest and perfectly immodest, like anybody else's.'

Almost as an aside, however, in his autobiography, he reveals that he considered orchestration as 'the branch in which Nadia Boulanger's teaching was less than perfect'.

Aaron Copland said that two qualities made her unique, namely her consuming love for music, and her ability to inspire a pupil with confidence in his own creative powers. In his case this received a very practical expression in Nadia Boulanger's commissioning of an organ concerto from Copland for her first American tour.

Not long after Nadia Boulanger was discovered by the

Americans, an Englishman, Lennox Berkeley, found his way to her through the recommendation of Maurice Ravel. In a way it is unfortunate that Berkeley is glibly labelled 'the most French of English composers', because labels have a tendency to stick, and they are often taken merely at face value. People tend not to look more closely at the product, and so the handy term of reference gains currency.

It is true in Lennox Berkeley's case that he has a lot of French blood in him, which may have given him something of the French temperament, but it would be hard to point to anything in his music that is specifically French. Certain qualities in his technique are reminiscent of Poulenc, notably a brilliance and elegance, an almost epigrammatic quality to the writing, and a delicate, if not iridescent, harmonic texture – and these we associate with the French character. But they are not exclusively French attributes.

The whole question of nationality, and nationalism in music, needs a very sensitive approach. Some composers have deliberately used readily recognizable national characteristics either to give their country's music stronger personality, or as a deliberate pastiche. Puccini's operas *Madame Butterfly* and *Turandot* exemplify the latter. There is also a nationalism that goes much deeper, where a composer's musical roots are in his native soil, and he does not have to use folk tunes to prove it.

When writing of the music of Ralph Vaughan Williams in 1931, Aaron Copland said: 'It is fairly safe to predict that Vaughan Williams will be the kind of local composer who stands for something great in the musical development of his own country but whose actual musical contribution cannot bear exportation . . . His is the music of a gentleman-farmer, noble in inspiration, but dull.' In all fairness to Aaron Copland, he later revised this opinion, particularly in view of such works as Vaughan Williams' fourth symphony, written only four years later, in 1935. Even so, many English people, along with Aaron Copland, would probably bracket Vaughan Williams with Elgar as two of the most English composers of all time. One only has to think of Vaughan Williams' *Fantasia on Greensleeves* (1908), the *Fantasia on a theme of Thomas Tallis* (1909), and the overture to the play *The Wasps* by Aristophanes of the same year, with its long sweeping melody that proclaims its Englishness in every note, to appreciate this fact. Yet Vaughan Williams at one time studied with Ravel, and even if he was in no way influenced by him, he must have been aware of what Ravel was seeking in his music. In fact, later in his career, Vaughan Williams was writing music that came much closer to Ravel's in his *Serenade to Music* of 1938 while never abandoning his English roots. One thinks here of the incomparable settings of Shakespeare songs of 1951, in which the eight-part writing is of almost impressionistic rhythmic and harmonic fluidity, or the exotic orchestration of his ninth and last symphony of 1958.

In the last analysis the essential is that the composer should be himself, which is what Nadia Boulanger has always advocated throughout her teaching career. Whenever a pupil has been strong in one particular department, she has been quick to recognize the fact. She did not make Lennox Berkeley do harmony exercises because she felt that his harmonic sense was perfectly adequate when he came to her. George Gershwin had met Ravel in New York and the French composer gave him a letter of introduction to Nadia Boulanger. Gershwin wanted to study with Ravel, but Ravel refused, telling him, 'You would only lose the spontaneous quality of your melody, and end by writing bad Ravel.' Nadia Boulanger also declined, for the same reason.

A budding composer cannot afford to be strong in one field only. He must know how to use all the tools of his trade, and Nadia Boulanger equips him with whatever is lacking. She is well qualified to do so, and despite the fact that she abandoned composition herself, it was, and has remained, her very life. There were her composing pupils, and there were her composer friends, either from her family connections or her own student days, or those she met through friends and to whom she was naturally attracted. Into this category falls the man who was arguably one of the most influential composers of the twentieth century, Igor Stravinsky. It was indeed providential that he should have come into Nadia Boulanger's career at such an important stage in its development – in the early 1920s.

2

Stravinsky,
and the Twenties

Igor Stravinsky was born in 1882 at Oranienbaum near St Petersburg – where Nadia Boulanger's mother was born. Despite the fact that his father was a famous singer at the Maryinsky Theatre – renowned for his bass voice and acting ability – he did not want his son to follow him, certainly not in that branch of his profession, and so Igor studied law, obtaining his diploma in 1905. Already, however, he knew that he wanted to be a composer, and when he had finished his studies, Rimsky-Korsakov, then Director of the Conservatory, took him under his wing for the next three years. Up to this point his writing had shown no particular originality, but two works of 1908 – *Scherzo fantastique* and *Feu d'artifice*, both for orchestra – gave some indication of what was to come. In fact it was hearing the second of these two works that inspired Diaghilev to commission a ballet from Stravinsky for the second season of his famous Ballets Russes in Paris. Stravinsky was working on an opera, *Le rossignol*, at the time, but set it aside for the new work, *The Firebird*, which brought the composer overnight success in 1910. He followed it the next year with *Petrushka*.

One feels with *Firebird* that Rimsky-Korsakov is still somewhere at his pupil's elbow, but in *Petrushka* the very personal rhythms, the use of folk tunes and the orchestration reveal Stravinsky as a composer in his own right, at the start of what is termed for convenience his Russian period. By way of contrast with these two ballets, two poems by Verlaine attracted Stravinsky at this time, and he set them to music, almost by way of relaxation, much in the same way as Benjamin Britten has

tended to write a small work on completion of a major one.*
Although he regarded the later work *Persephone* (1933–4) as his
first real exercise in setting a French text, the Verlaine songs
show how much Stravinsky looked towards France at this
period, where his music was probably heard more than in his
native Russia.

Nadia Boulanger, always very much aware of what was
going on in the musical world, was of course bound to come into
contact with Stravinsky sooner or later. He was also Russian,
which was a considerable point in his favour. Considering how
important Stravinsky was to become to Nadia, one of her earliest published references to him is interesting. On 26 January
1919 *Firebird* and *Feu d'Artifice* were given in Paris at one of the
Colonne-Lamoureux concerts. Her comments were barely restrained: 'Stravinsky, with the boldness of innovators and
extraordinary orchestral virtuosity, translates the most spontaneous movement, that which brings nature closest to the
primitive state . . .' On 23 February of that year, in the same
series of concerts, *Petrushka* was also given.

The reference to 'the primitive state' almost inevitably harks
back to 29 May 1913, when *The Rite of Spring* was unleashed
upon the audience assembled in the Théâtre des
Champs-Elysées in Paris, where Debussy's *Jeux* had received
its première, with the same company, only two weeks earlier.
Here is Gertrude Stein's account of the event from *The Autobiography of Alice B. Toklas*:

'The performance began. No sooner had it commenced when the
excitement began. The scene now so well known with its brilliantly
coloured background now not at all extraordinary, outraged the
Paris audience. No sooner did the music begin and the dancing
than they began to hiss. The defenders began to applaud. We could
hear nothing, as a matter of fact I never did hear any of the music of
the Sacre du Printemps because it was the only time I ever saw it
and one literally could not, throughout the whole performance,
hear the sound of music. The dancing was very fine and that we
could see although our attention was constantly distracted by a

* The songs were titled from the collections of Verlaine's poems published
as *La Bonne Chanson* and *Sagesse*. The actual poems are *La lune blanche luit dans les
bois* and *Le son du cor*. The piano accompaniments were orchestrated by Stravinsky in 1953.

man in the box next to us flourishing his cane, and finally in a vio-
lent altercation with an enthusiast in the box next to him, his cane
came down and smashed the opera hat the other had just put on in
defiance. It was all incredibly fierce.'

Romola Nijinsky, in her book *Nijinsky*, confirms that the
music could not even be heard on the stage, and that it was only
Nijinsky, beating time from the wings, who kept the dancers
going. Despite the furore, she maintained that the beauty of the
dance of the Chosen Maiden was such that the unruly audience
was disarmed. Stravinsky, however, in his *Chroniques de ma vie*,
was less appreciative of Nijinsky's choreography:

> 'The general impression of this choreography I had then, and
> have kept until today, is the irresponsibility with which it was
> devised by Nijinsky. It clearly revealed his incapacity to assimilate
> and appropriate to himself the revolutionary idea that constituted
> Diaghilev's creed, and which the latter had persistently and labori-
> ously inculcated into him. The choreography showed a very painful
> effort without result rather than a plastic, simple and natural reali-
> zation unfolding the music's intentions. How far all this was from
> what I had desired!'

Stravinsky may have disliked the dancing, but not so the
audience; they were not concerned one way or the other by the
choreography, it was the music they found alarming. For some
of them the seeming chaos must have been one with the chaos of
Schönberg's *Pierrot Lunaire* (1911), which had been heard for
the first time in Berlin the year before. It is true that Stravinsky
had heard *Pierrot Lunaire* on 8 December 1912 in Berlin, and
some of its influence may be traceable in his work from that
period. Subsequent analysis, however, would reveal that
whereas Schönberg was definitely extending the breakdown of
tonality in *Pierrot Lunaire*, Stravinsky was building his complex
polyphony on traditional harmonies in *The Rite of Spring*, and
the polytonality of the work was in fact strengthening tonality.

What most appealed to Nadia Boulanger in Stravinsky's
music, as she wrote some years later, was the fact that it satisfied one's mental faculties, and yet at the same time touched the
heart. This, for her, was the touchstone of good music, and the
delicate balance that she always sought to inculcate in her
pupils' music. Taken to its furthest extent, it sums up her ideal
of life, too.

But this did not make Stravinsky's work any less revolutionary, since it called seriously into question what had been the accepted canons of what was until then musically beautiful. He showed that what is artistically fine need not necessarily have to be Romantic and refined, and his 'Tableaux of Pagan Russia', as *The Rite* was subtitled, rediscovered in Slav folklore a vigorous, primitive form of art.

In 1914, while returning from a visit to Russia, Stravinsky was caught in Switzerland by the outbreak of hostilities between France and Germany. From Stravinsky's stay in Switzerland during World War One came *Les Noces*, though it was not choreographed until 1923, and *The Soldier's Tale*. The Bolshevik Revolution of 1917 had brought to an end the life he had known in Russia and also the Russian period in his music. He made a brief excursion into jazz with *Ragtime* and *Piano Rag Music* (1918–19), but if he was looking for a style that would transcend national characteristics, it was not to be found here.

In fact the inspiration came from Diaghilev, and Stravinsky returned to classicism by taking the music of Pergolesi (1710–36) for a new ballet, *Pulcinella* (1919–20). By the same token one may regard the concerto for piano and orchestra (1922–4), as well as the piano sonata (1924), as a return to Bach, though there was the additional factor that at this time Stravinsky was attempting to earn money as a concert pianist and conductor, and he wanted to write something of his own for his repertoire.

In some respects the culmination of this neoclassical period may be regarded as *Oedipus Rex*, an opera-oratorio written in 1926–7 in collaboration with Jean Cocteau. As an example of the cross-fertilization that existed among this group of artists and musicians, it is interesting that Nadia Boulanger, writing in February 1947 about the recording of Stravinsky's Ebony Concerto, recalled Cocteau's remark that an original artist was incapable of copying; he therefore only had to copy to be original. What appealed most to Nadia Boulanger at this point was that through submitting himself to all the demands of writing in this neoclassical idiom, Stravinsky had emerged with a totally new creation.

One must not imagine that all Stravinsky's writing at

this time was in the same idiom, however, for alongside the neoclassical works are others such as *Mavra* (1922) and *Le baiser de la fée* (1928), which have Romantic tendencies that are almost redolent of Tchaikovsky by comparison, not to mention what one might term the baroque nature of *Apollo musagetes* (1927–8) and *Capriccio* (1929), or the hieratic nature of the Symphony of Psalms (1930) and *Persephone* (1933–4). Again, a different style or idiom is found in the memorial to Debussy – *Symphonies pour instruments à vent* (1920) – and the *Concertino* for string quartet of the same year. The unifying concept in all his music until his opera *The Rake's Progress* in 1951 was 'the musical model', and this is particularly true of the twenty years he spent in Paris.

Many factors contributed to Stravinsky's decision to settle in Paris. As long before as 1889 Rimsky-Korsakov, his teacher, had gone there to conduct a concert of his works during the Universal Exposition. It was from Paris that Diaghilev had commissioned *The Firebird*, and it was there in 1913 that *The Rite of Spring* had had its *succès de scandale*. There were other, less dramatic factors, such as the period of collaboration with Ravel that same year at Clareus on Lake Geneva, when they reorchestrated Mussorgsky's *Khovantchina*, and the fact that Ravel's *Daphnis and Chloë* was commissioned for Diaghilev's Ballets Russes and first given in 1912, the year before *The Rite of Spring*. When the combination of war and revolution made a return to Russia impossible, France seemed the automatic place in which to settle, and Stravinsky described it as his second motherland.

However much he travelled after the war, and he covered much of Western Europe at this time, Paris was always his base, as it was for so much of the artistic world of the Twenties. In Paris there was the possibility of having one's work recognized, and there was a considerable body of informed critics and connoisseurs. There was also a good deal of patronage available. Almost inevitably this led to factions and rivalry, some of it regrettable in its side effects. People tended to find themselves classified as belonging to such and such a group almost without knowing it. On the other hand, there were certain very closely knit groups that tended to be exclusive. At its best it was a meeting of people of similar views cutting right across partisanship, and some managed to belong to several groups. The effect was thus one of interlocking circles rather than isolated entities, which is obviously a much healthier state of affairs.

Even so, there is a limit to the number of friends people can have, and when a person finds himself excluded from any particular group, he is bound to resent the fact. In these circumstances it is hard not to feel that such exclusion is deliberate, and it was particularly difficult for some of the foreigners drawn to Paris to gain admission to the recognized groups. When there was a ready-made connection, such as the Diaghilev one, it was relatively easy for a Stravinsky to gain an *entrée*.

As well as the incoming foreigners, there were plenty of aspiring young French men and women who also wanted to make their way in the world. Some came to the fore of their own accord, but whether French or foreign, virtually all needed the support of friends and promoters. In addition to her budding friendship with Stravinsky, Nadia Boulanger made friends with a number of rich and influential – and also, let it be said, often talented – members of the French aristocracy. Detractors have cynically called her *La petite soeur des riches* (the little sister of the rich), punning on the religious order known as the Little Sisters of the Poor. In view of the aristocratic family on her mother's side, the jibe was not only unfair, but inaccurate. Of these friends, the Polignacs were probably the most important.

Princesse Edmond de Polignac, who was the American Winnaretta Singer before her marriage, was an early patron of Stravinsky. While the composer was in Switzerland during World War One, Diaghilev had arranged a gala at the Paris Opéra in aid of the Red Cross, in the course of which Stravinsky was to conduct his own *Firebird*. Before leaving Paris for Switzerland, he took the opportunity of seeing some of his friends, and in particular the Princesse de Polignac, who wanted 'a little piece for drawing-room presentation', which she envisaged putting on as soon as the war was over. Stravinsky suggested *Renard* to her, since he had already sketched it out. She liked the idea, and so he began to work on it as soon as he got back to Switzerland.

It was June 1922 before *Renard* was finally given its first performance at the Paris Opéra, thanks to the generosity of the

Princesse de Polignac. Nijinsky's sister Bronislava choreographed it, Larionov designed the scenery and the costumes,
and Ansermet conducted. Although Stravinsky was very happy
with the production itself, he was unhappy at its placing in the
programme, and the resultant disapproval of the critics.

Almost exactly a year later *Les Noces* was given its first performance in Paris, this time at the Gaîté Lyrique. There was a
private preview at the Princesse de Polignac's, and this became
almost an established pattern. Certainly it was true of *The
Soldier's Tale*, the concerto for piano and orchestra, the sonata
for piano (which was dedicated to the princess) and *Oedipus Rex*,
which she also helped finance.

It was the conductor Koussevitsky who suggested that Stravinsky should play the piano part of his concerto himself, and
although at first Stravinsky did not think that he was up to it, he
worked very hard at his technique so as to reach the necessary
standard in time. A week before its première at a Koussevitsky
concert at the Paris Opéra on 22 May 1924, Stravinsky played
it at the Princesse de Polignac's, Jean Weiner providing the orchestral parts on a second piano. When it came to the actual
performance, Stravinsky had a sudden lapse of memory before
the opening of the Largo. He simply could not remember how
the piano solo began. Luckily Koussevitsky was able to whisper
the notes to him and so continue the performance.

Koussevitsky's name runs like a thread through this period
and this particular group of musicians. Born near Tver in
Russia in 1874, he died at Boston in 1951. He was a virtuoso
double-bass player, and in the earlier part of his career did
much to bring contemporary music to the fore by publishing it.
Later he concentrated more on conducting it and commissioning it, particularly while he was conductor of the Boston
Symphony Orchestra, from 1924 to 1949, an appointment for
which Virgil Thomson takes most of the credit upon himself. In
1947 he created the Natalie Koussevitsky Foundation as a
memorial to his first wife, with the aim, among others, of commissioning new works from composers on both sides of the
Atlantic. His second wife, Olga, continued the work of the foundation after his death.

Aaron Copland first met Koussevitsky in Paris in the spring
of 1923, when Nadia Boulanger took Copland to his apartment

soon after Koussevitsky's new appointment to Boston had been announced. While living in Paris, Koussevitsky gave a series of concerts that bore his name at the Paris Opéra each spring and autumn. Many new works had their first auditions at these concerts, and it was an astute move on Nadia Boulanger's part to take the young Copland to meet him, since he was soon to go to the country of her pupil's birth. Copland took with him the manuscript of a piece entitled *Cortège macabre*, which was an excerpt from a ballet he was then working on under the eye of Nadia Boulanger. Copland played the piece through for him, and Koussevitsky promised to have it performed in the course of his first season in Boston.

Naturally, for such a young composer, there was the thrill of having a work performed by a famous conductor and a famous orchestra, but a first performance was not the most important, as Copland very soon came to appreciate. In fact he deplored the then very prevalent tendency in America in the early Twenties to concentrate on first performances. When a work had been performed once, it seemed to be destined for oblivion. Even if it was well received in one town, there was little or no chance that it would be performed in another, let alone in another country. This was bad enough, but, when coupled with the fact that many conductors and orchestral players really had little appetite for contemporary music, the result was often a half-hearted performance that did not even begin to do the work justice. Such an attitude naturally communicated itself to the audience, who, in the circumstances, could hardly be expected to be won over.

With the advent of Koussevitsky to Boston, the picture changed dramatically. He believed in the new music he conducted – as he had in Russia with Scriabin, Stravinsky and Prokofiev and in Paris with Ravel, Honegger and others. When the Boston Symphony Orchestra celebrated its fiftieth anniversary in 1930, Koussevitsky commissioned a symphony from Stravinsky, which proved to be the Symphony of Psalms. Koussevitsky himself has said of the composer's role:

'Every great, or less great, or even little, composer brings something to the art of music which makes the art great in its entirety. Each one brings his portion. In examination of his music we can see how real a composer is. We can see whether his technique is perfect; whether he knows how the orchestra and the individual instruments sound and whether or not he has something to say, no matter what the degree of importance. Sometimes a single man has one single word to say in all his life and that one word may be as important as the lifework of a great genius. We need that word – and so does the genius himself need that word.'

Of course Stravinsky was only one of the composers making a name for himself at the time. Some are now completely forgotten, others have turned from composing to conducting, others simply failed to live up to their promise or expectations. Fauré and Saint-Saëns, as well as D'Indy, were still alive in 1921. Ravel, Satie, Schmitt and Dukas were at the height of their powers, and Milhaud and Poulenc were under thirty and under twenty respectively.

Darius Milhaud (1892–1970) was especially important in the musical Paris of the Twenties, though he may not have stood up to the passage of time as well as some imagined he would in those days. At that time, when the music he wrote for Paul Claudel's *Protée* was first heard, people thought that Milhaud was mad. He was in fact something of an *enfant terrible* of French music in those days, belonging to the group known as Les Six – Germaine Tailleferre, Louis Durey, Georges Auric, Francis Poulenc and Arthur Honegger. Jean Cocteau was artist 'by appointment' to this group, and to celebrate the fact he drew a symbolic composite sketch of the profiles of all six composers with himself at the centre. Virgil Thomson described the group:

'The chief go-between for artists and hostesses was Jean Cocteau – poet, playwright, and impeccable theatre workman. He could launch a fashion, guide a career, organize its social and financial backing. And his main protectorate in music, the group that he had publicized so powerfully after World War I that they came to share condominium with him in the salons, were four composers out of the well-known Group of Six – Milhaud, Honegger, Auric and Poulenc.'

Added to this group of influential composers, though in fact standing completely on his own, is the strange figure of Erik Satie. He is one of the few composers that Nadia

Boulanger allowed herself to criticize outright in public, which she did in an article published in 1923, where she described the music of his *Parade* as vulgar. Gide had seen the ballet itself in January 1921. His remark in his diary was to the effect that one did not know what to admire most, the pretension or the poverty of the work. Picasso and Cocteau had combined with Satie on the ballet, and it may have been a case of professional jealousy on Gide's part. Stravinsky also saw it during this season of the Diaghilev ballet in the winter of 1920–21, but whereas Gide simply found it pretentious and, presumably, impoverished, it very much appealed to Stravinsky:

> 'Although I had played the music on the piano, seen photographs of the scenery and costumes, and was intimately acquainted with the scenario, the performance gave me the impression of freshness and real originality. *Parade* confirmed me still further in my conviction of Satie's merit in the part he had played in French music by opposing to the vagueness of a decrepit impressionism a precise and firm language stripped of all pictorial embellishments.'

Only now are we witnessing a reappraisal of Satie's role and his importance in the history of French music. At present his standing is high, because his aesthetic appeals to the aesthetic of a certain section of contemporary music-lovers; after World War Two his stock was low – in fact virtually nil. Presumably the pendulum will come to rest somewhere in between. Certainly there is no question that Satie was important to several musicians and artists, because he stimulated them in a way it is difficult to appreciate unless one was there at the time, or fully understands all the influences that were at play. He was important to Virgil Thomson, for whom his music was the test of how truly a composer was a child of the twentieth century. Thomson later became a promoter of Satie's music – in particular *Socrate*, which is certainly one of his more substantial works. But as Thomson quite openly admits, people take to Satie or they don't – as to Gertrude Stein. Certainly in this context one can see the distinction between the Gide world and that of Thomson and Stein, and why there was relatively little sympathy.

Virgil Thomson rather resented not being admitted to the

musical power group, as he termed it. He had his own titled lady patron, however, in the Duchesse de Clermont-Tonnerre, and in 1927 his cantata *Capital Capitals* was performed at a costume party at her house in the rue Raynouard.

Mauriac described the Duchesse as bearing down on her guests with her lorgnette, as if she were some animal of prey deciding whether they were edible or not. The French journalist Robert de Saint Jean attended one of her evenings towards the end of May 1928, and thought that she looked like a Viking under her tiara, as she went from group to group assuring her guests that the attraction of the evening, the singer Yvonne Georges, was bound to arrive soon. The singer eventually appeared at ten minutes past midnight, much to everyone's relief, but not least that of Mme de Clermont-Tonnerre, who had begun to perspire. M. Gandarillas, the inveterate party-goer, convinced that Yvonne Georges had forgotten the engagement, had already left, and his hostess had been too distraught to prevent him.

In such circumstances it was not surprising that the poor singer was nervous, and the guests hostile. Not satisfied with the amount of applause, Mme de Clermont-Tonnerre went from room to room, stimulating enthusiasm. As she was passing one group she overheard someone say:

"'I couldn't hear the words very well.'"
"'To whom are you referring?' demanded the irate hostess.
"'We were talking about *La Duse*' [the Italian actress Eleonora Duse, who had died in 1924].'

There were encores, after which the guests began to take their leave, mumbling excuses. The hostess protested that it was much too early to go, especially as the next day was a holiday. Someone invented an early train to catch, and as the writer Julien Green approached to take his leave, before he had even opened his mouth, the Duchesse attacked him with the suggestion that he, too, must have a train to catch. To those who were afraid to leave she announced joyfully that they would have something to drink, the poor woman would sing once more, and then they would have some supper. Yvonne Georges was, by this time, exhausted.

Whenever the Duchesse's name was mentioned in front of

Marthe Bibesco, she quoted a sentence from the Duchesse's memoirs about her childhood: 'Over-saturated in luxury, I soon became *blasée* about monetary manipulation.' Nor did Mme de Clermont-Tonnerre endear herself to the admirers of Paul Valéry – to whom Nadia Boulanger was devoted – by allowing herself to be quoted in *Vogue* to the effect that there had been a Valéry crash, as in Wall Street. 'In spite of that,' she continued, 'I read him.' Virginia Woolf she pronounced to be simply boring: '*Quelle raseuse!*'

At this time Gertrude Stein was trying to find a patron for Thomson, and through the sculptor Jo Davidson he was introduced to Elsa Maxwell. Miss Maxwell was to take Thomson's career in hand, and the crowning event of it was to be a performance of his opera at Monte Carlo in the spring of 1929. Needless to say, none of this materialized. Neither did Miss Maxwell, towards the end of this somewhat brief encounter. Cocteau offered to write to the Princesse de Polignac on Thomson's behalf, but Thomson declined, suspecting that his name had never even been mentioned to her.

By contrast, Igor Markevitch's success with the Princess annoyed Thomson, since he sensed that he could have been taken up if the Polignac circle had so wished. As he wrote of that time, about 1928: 'my music, my career, my position in the whole time-and-place setup was something the French power group did not choose to handle. I was not being suppressed, not for the present; that effort was to be made four years later. But certainly I was not being adopted.' He was well aware that the commissions other composers then in Paris were receiving from Diaghilev and the Princesse de Polignac were not coming his way. In the long run it was probably as well for his own development, for it kept him an American composer, and not, as he described it, 'a pseudo-Gallic clinger-on'.

Now known more as a conductor, Markevitch was included by Virgil Thomson as one of the School of Paris composers in the early 1930s, along with Nicolas Nabokov and Vittorio Rieti. In fact Thomson's autobiography gives a somewhat acid aperçu of Markevitch's career specifically in connection with a concert of Thomson's works given in Paris in 1931:

'To this concert came, looking for evidence, the new boy-genius

Igor Markevitch. This Russian of barely twenty had been discovered some three years earlier, in 1928, by Diaghilev, then launched by Cocteau, taken up as a cause by Nadia Boulanger, blessed by Henri Prunières, patronized by the Princesse de Polignac, and endowed by the Vicomtesse de Noailles.'

By his own admission, Thomson was slow to make friends when he might have done so in the musical world of Paris between the wars, and although one can appreciate why he felt that he could not do so if this compromised his artistic integrity, the theme recurs quite frequently in his autobiography, implying not only that he felt he ought to have been accepted by that world, but also that it was worth his while to be accepted. Certainly it would have been so financially at that time, though whether artistically as well is very much open to discussion. He seems to take some consolation from the fact that one of his articles, which received wide distribution, virtually put an end to Igor Markevitch's composing career, despite the fact that Thomson had not meant it to be so devastating at the time.

This bitter tit-for-tat has always existed between artists, and is all the more regrettable because of the heights to which art may aspire. In this case Thomson had expressed reservations about Markevitch's music; and Markevitch had heard about it, and dismissed Thomson's Violin Sonata as being merely César Franck. Thomson replied later by writing in an article that, along with George Antheil, Markevitch was more interesting for his career than his composition, and this was thought to have dissuaded Koussevitsky from conducting some of Markevitch's music. This may or may not be so, but Koussevitsky was always a devoted champion of new music and had his own views on the matter – sufficiently so, in fact, to reject a piece of Virgil Thomson's as unsuitable for performance. Possibly Thomson felt that Koussevitsky owed him a debt for his glowing report, written in 1922, of Koussevitsky's concerts at the Paris Opéra, which, Thomson thought, gained Koussevitsky the musical directorship of the Boston Symphony Orchestra, in succession to Pierre Monteux.

It is one of the hard facts of being an artist in any field that recognition is not always a guarantee of quality, and vice versa. Every artist has to be philosophical about it and carry on

nevertheless. Needless to say, this requires considerable courage at times when success is elusive, as well as acute discernment when it comes easily.

Moreover, living as we do in the wake of Romanticism, many
listeners, if not critics, still regard inspiration a *sine qua non*, and
music as 'good' only if it touches them and is in some way 'significant' for them. Certain composers, however, regard the
writing of music as a job like any other. Tchaikovsky and Stravinsky felt this way, as do Copland and Britten. In fact it is interesting that Stravinsky in his autobiography should quote a
letter of Tchaikovsky's saying just this:

> 'Since I began to compose I have made it my object to be, in my
> craft, what the most illustrious masters were in theirs; that is to say,
> I wanted to be, like them, an artisan, just as a shoemaker is . . .
> (They) composed their immortal works exactly as a shoemaker
> makes shoes; that is to say, day in, day out, and for the most part to
> order.'

Such a viewpoint might shock the average concertgoer, who
likes to think that composers are, at least for their greatest
works, in some way 'inspired'. Not that this is to suggest that
craftsmanship and inspiration in composition are mutually exclusive, by any means. Indeed, the two are inextricably inter-
twined. The amount of sheer craftsmanship, however, is
probably much greater than many would imagine, and this is
why Nadia Boulanger feels that musicians ought to make composition a natural function.

Then again, the Romantic period tended to make some imagine that all music had to be 'great' or 'significant'. Naturally
no one would wish to be subjected to second-rate music all the
time, but then how capable is one of listening to even a whole
concert of 'great' music with all the concentration it deserves?
In these days of long-playing records, cassettes, broadcasting
and television, we are accustomed to masterpieces at the touch
of a switch. We automatically assume that all music competes
with that of the giants. What then of the accomplished composer who serves the community but fails to achieve 'greatness'? Again, the Romantic notion of the composer in his ivory
tower has done the profession a great disservice, from which it
has only slowly emerged. Very few composers, if any, can have

consciously composed for 'greatness'. Most are satisfied with the feeling that their work 'came off' in performance – in other words that it got across to the audience. Even if the listeners liked only part of the work, at least the composer has achieved something. As Aaron Copland wrote:

> 'Nothing pleases the composer so much as to have people disagree as to the movements of his piece that they liked best. If there is enough disagreement, it means that everyone liked something best – which is just what the composer wants to hear. The fact that this might include other parts that no one liked never seems to matter.'

Ravel once said to Georges Auric that he would have liked to write a work on orchestration illustrated by examples of his own works that had failed to 'come off'. When Nadia Boulanger went to compliment Ravel on his orchestration the morning after the first performance of *Bolero* (1928), he seemed rather sad that it had been so successful, when his *Chansons madécasses*, about which he felt much more keenly, had not. Musically speaking, the *Chansons madécasses* are incomparably more significant than *Bolero*, though the latter is of course a remarkable achievement by any standards. These orchestrated songs were unfortunately somewhat ahead of their time, though one sees this now with the benefit of hindsight. Ravel had clashed with the musical establishment before, so he knew what it was not to be understood, and he was by no means an evangelizing composer. He found his musical self and remained true to it.

Inexorably, however, in the Twenties and Thirties French music was running out of steam, and despite the fact that the post-Romantic French composers inspired other nations musically, they failed to hand on anything very much of value to France itself. Today one can count the French composers of any note on the fingers on one hand. Indeed French musical life is in a parlous state.

Herein lies an answer to the question as to why Nadia Boulanger has had so few French pupils of note. She was herself part of the last great flowering of French music, and there have been few to follow on. At one time it seemed as if Igor Markevitch might take up the flag, particularly at the première of his ballet *Icare* (1933), and in some ways Jean Françaix did; but Olivier Messiaen and Pierre Boulez have been the only composers to make any deep impression outside or even inside France. Even Boulez seems to have run out of steam, at least for the time being, and now devotes himself mostly to conducting. Minimal patronage in a highly centralized and state-controlled musical establishment, and the virtual disappearance of private patrons in post-World War Two France, have made the composer's life even more difficult.

There was a postscript to the Thomson-Polignac non-affair that had a certain kind of poetic justice. After World War Two Thomson went to Venice to stay with the distinguished pianist Prince George Chavchavadze and his wife, in an apartment consisting of two floors of the palazzo that had belonged to the late Princesse de Polignac. Gian Francesco Malipiero, Director of the Conservatoire, gave Thomson Wagner's baton to hold. Thomson said that he felt he had touched electricity.

Back in the Twenties, a more significant event for Thomson than the drawing-room concerts was the concert devised by Nadia Boulanger in 1926 devoted exclusively to the young American composers Herbert Elwell, Aaron Copland, Walter Piston, Theodore Chanler, George Antheil and Thomson himself. There is a remarkable photograph taken at the time of this concert of the first three composers named and Thomson, in Nadia Boulanger's apartment, which has altered remarkably little in the last fifty years or so.

Three years later, in 1929, there was another concert by young American composers, paid for with money that Aaron Copland had brought from a patroness in New York. This time, in addition to music by Thomson and Copland, the concert included works by Roy Harris and Israel Citkowitz – also Boulanger pupils at that time – and Carlos Chávez. In the circumstances it was a generous gesture on Boulanger's part, since she mobilized an audience of international standing in the then modern-musical world, and was not especially enthusiastic at the way Thomson's music was developing at that time. In a letter to Gertrude Stein after the concert Virgil Thomson said that he imagined he had been intended as comic relief, whereas in fact he had almost stolen the show. This would not please Nadia Boulanger, he suspected.

The Twenties were ending. A sign that new ideas and a new spirit were abroad was there for all to see. The whole environment was undergoing radical changes, and as an indication that at least some people were aware of the fact, in June 1929 the Vicomte and Vicomtesse de Noailles gave their famous *bal des matières*, when all the guests were to dress in such materials as plastic, glass, metal or even straw – so long as it evoked modern times. Two months later, far off in Venice, Serge Diaghilev passed away, and, as Virgil Thomson rightly remarks, it was this event more than anything else that signified the ending of an epoch.

3

The Thirties

Shifts of loyalty, realignment of groups, and changes in vision were characteristic of the change from Twenties to Thirties. Typical was perhaps the way in which Gide succeeded Cocteau as Stravinsky's partner at the turn of the decade. Gide was very happy at the prospect of working with Stravinsky. They had both been at Saas Fee in Switzerland back in August 1917, when Stravinsky recommended Tolstoy's *Journal* to Gide. Gide and Stravinsky subsequently discussed possible collaboration – on Shakespeare's *Antony and Cleopatra*, which Gide had translated – as is apparent from the comments Gide made after attending a performance of Cocteau's version of Sophocles' *Antigone* in Paris in January 1923. But Cocteau and Stravinsky were at that time artistically much of the same mind, and were soon to work on *Oedipus Rex* (1926–7).

In 1933 Gide was to have his turn, when he went to Wiesbaden with Ida Rubinstein to discuss with Stravinsky the new work *Persephone*, Gide's translation of a Homeric hymn to Demeter. Certainly, comparing Gide's reference in his *Journal* and that of Stravinsky in his autobiography (1936), the two seem to have had an excellent working relationship. For Stravinsky it was the first time he had set French to music, apart from two songs to words of Verlaine from an earlier period.

However, when it came to the performance at the Paris Opéra, Stravinsky was much less happy. Gide failed to appear at rehearsals or at any of the three performances on 30 April, 4 May and 9 May 1934, Stravinsky was not consulted about the scenery, and it was only the work of the choreographer Kurt Jooss that seemed to give Stravinsky any consolation. Gide's

Journal significantly made no reference to this part of the venture at all.

Really Stravinsky need hardly have worried. By this time his international reputation was well assured, and although it is never very satisfactory to be forced to accept adverse criticism of one's work, the slipshod Paris performances of *Persephone* were cancelled out by a much more satisfactory interpretation in London soon after. The friendships he had formed also helped Stravinsky to be somewhat philosophical, and in particular the support given by such tried and trusted friends as the Polignacs, musical professionals such as Koussevitsky, and especially that of Nadia Boulanger.

For Nadia Boulanger herself this was a time of rewarding friendships, and her own relations with the Polignac family were particularly fruitful. On 30 June 1933, for example, Nadia organized a recital at the home of the Princesse de Polignac in the rue Cortembert, at which the Princesse Edmond played the piano and Comtesse Jean (Marie-Blanche) sang. It was Marie-Blanche who was to become one of the singers in Nadia Boulanger's ensemble for the famous Monteverdi recording. The association also helped pupils such as Jean Françaix, whose chamber comic opera *Le diable boiteux* was first heard at the Polignacs' in 1937.

From a musical point of view, however, the most important friendship of her career in these years was that with Stravinsky, and it came as no surprise when it was announced in *Le Monde Musical* for 30 September 1935 that Nadia Boulanger and Stravinsky were to give composition classes at the Ecole Normale, in succession to Paul Dukas. Stravinsky became a naturalized Frenchman in 1936, the year in which he was also a candidate for the Académie des Beaux-Arts, but had to give way to Florent Schmitt.

The first programmes for Nadia Boulanger's choral and analysis classes, held at her home, were announced at this time, too. They reveal the extraordinary breadth of her musical culture. Running from November to June, they left her free to teach at the American Conservatory at Fontainebleau in July and August. The programme for the 1935–6 series included Bach (St John Passion), Monteverdi, Hindemith, Schütz, Stravinsky (*Persephone*), Carissimi (*Jephthah*), Palestrina, Taverner,

Tallis, Lotti, Cavalieri, Debussy, Binchois and Françaix. The next year Bach's St Matthew Passion replaced the St John and Stravinsky's *Noces* replaced *Persephone*, but the basic mixture remained the same. The years 1938–9 marked the inclusion of Schubert and Purcell – the latter a particularly enlightened addition, when he was still relatively little known even in his native England, but then the same might be said of Taverner and Tallis also. Twenty-four years later (1962–3) the menu was still much the same – Bach, Bartók, Buxtehude, Chopin, Debussy, Fauré, Françaix, Monteverdi, Mozart, Perotin, Poulenc, Ravel, Schubert, Schumann, Stravinsky and Webern, and the courses still lasted from November to June.

During this period her friendship with Paul Valéry also developed, and she still keeps his photograph, dedicated in 1928 'to Nadia Boulanger, who gives enthusiasm through rigour'. Elsewhere he wrote identifying her with 'enthusiasm and order, which are the two symmetrical powers of [the] great art'. Valéry wrote a charming letter to Alexis Léger in 1937, when Nadia Boulanger wanted to pay another visit to America. It was reproduced in the programme for the eightieth-birthday celebration at the Monte Carlo Opera House in 1967, and runs as follows:

'To Alexis Leger, Ambassadeur de France and Secretary General for Foreign Affairs.

'My dear friend,
Miss Nadia Boulanger, who wishes to talk to you about her next visit to America, imagines that she needs someone to introduce her to you, as if it were not Music in person (I mean the highest and most beautiful Music) who should come with her for an audience of you.

   'My role is somewhat vain. But it gives me the opportunity that is rare and even unique, of sending you my friendship through a person I admire . . .'

Paul Valéry (1871–1945) was possessed of an extremely wide culture, which was steeped in humanism. Under a basically classical form, especially in his poetry, he brought his great intelligence to bear on the anxieties and disquiet of the enquiring mind. He once wrote, 'I know where I am going, let me guide you'. To his admirers – and they were many – there was nothing at all extraordinary in this claim. If anyone was permitted to make it, it was Paul Valéry. Nadia Boulanger admired him enormously, finding in him inspiration and support for the role she had chosen to play in life. In return, his admiration for her was profound, and his death was a great loss to her.

The Twenties had been the decade in which Nadia Boulanger had established her base and consolidated her position, and in the Thirties she emerged as a figure of considerable weight in the musical world. Her teaching commitment alone was considerable, but in the Thirties Nadia Boulanger also gave numerous public performances, playing in two-piano recitals with Dinu Lipatti – then (in 1937) barely twenty years old – and including in the programme a polka by her pupil Lennox Berkeley. In 1938 she played with Clifford Curzon, again in a two-piano recital. This concert activity took her out of France regularly, but had to be combined with what was by now a heavy schedule of official teaching duties and private lessons.

However, she was also striking out as a conductor. In 1936 she conducted Fauré's *Requiem* in London, and in 1937 returned there to conduct the same work again. She made a habit of being the first woman to conduct several orchestras. She was the first woman to conduct at a Royal Philharmonic Concert in London, and the first to conduct the Boston Symphony Orchestra, the Philadelphia Orchestra and the New York Philharmonic. Even today not many women have followed in her steps, though there are certainly many more women working in music, especially as composers, and radio and television music producers. She conducted the first performance of Stravinsky's Dumbarton Oaks Concerto on 8 May 1938 in Washington, and he then described her as 'the person who hears everything' – such was the impression she made on him with her musical ear.

The previous year, 1937, had also been a memorable year, since she had then recorded the Monteverdi madrigals. Hugues Cuénod, who was one of the singers, had this to say:

'After the first year or two, I sometimes sang at her little courses on Bach, and I must say that if I have any style and any intelligence, and anything good in my singing, at the moment, it's very greatly to her that I owe it. We were a very nice little group and we had already done quite a lot of Monteverdi in small concerts in Paris, at the Cercle Interalliée and sometimes at the Radio, and in the few drawing-rooms and musical circles, and *La Voix de son Maître* asked Nadia Boulanger to record some, and it was the first time, I believe, that a lot of Monteverdi was recorded.'

Since then Monteverdi has become much more popular – as has a great deal of baroque and pre-classical music – so that to a contemporary ear the piano accompaniments provided by Nadia Boulanger for this record sound anachronistic. We now expect that a harpsichord will be used where necessary, but in those days it was a colossal achievement to have put any Monteverdi on to record at all. She was to do a similar thing with another recording, entitled *Petit Concert de Musique Française*, where technical anachronism is totally forgotten in the face of expert interpretation.

Cuénod got to know Nadia Boulanger in 1933 through a Finnish singer, Gertrud Alftan, who at that time sang in the German church in Paris. Nadia accompanied Hugues Cuénod, and he included some of her songs from time to time in his programmes, which she appreciated as a gesture from him, but did not really feel that they warranted public performance. In the three consecutive years from 1937 to 1939 he went with her to America, giving recitals, along with Doda Conrad, Paul Derenne and Marie-Blanche de Polignac.

The 1937 recording of the Monteverdi is one of the landmarks in the history of recording, and also in the history of Monteverdi's rediscovery, for which credit does not go entirely to Nadia Boulanger, as she would be the first to admit. Vincent d'Indy (1851–1931) had staged *Orfeo* before World War One and both *L'incoronazione di Poppea* and *Il ritorno d'Ulisse* shortly after it. What Nadia Boulanger did was to bring to popular notice the vast treasure-house of madrigals and other vocal and instrumental music by Monteverdi, and place it before the general public.

The foundation of the Schola Cantorum in the rue St Jacques (on the Left Bank) in 1894 by D'Indy, Charles Bordes and Félix Alexandre Guilmant (with whom Nadia Boulanger studied the organ) had been an important step in increasing the study of early music, and early French music in particular. D'Indy was the chief figure in this movement, and in thirty years he organized some 200 concerts of music by Charpentier, Rameau, Gluck and Bach. Not everyone found artistic merit in these concerts. Gide went to a performance of *Orfeo* at the Schola in 1906 and pronounced it very mediocre. From a scholarly point of view, Goldschmidt's editions are much more useful for modern scholars, because he contented himself with simply establishing accurate texts, with no attempt at editing.

D'Indy's *Traité de composition*, a mixture of mysticism and science, is in reality a resumé of his teaching at the Schola Cantorum. That teaching was sometimes too aggressive and too rigid, but nevertheless produced such highly individual composers as Roussel and Satie. Rather than regarding the rue Ballu as the opposing camp on the Right Bank, one should think of it as complementing and extending what was then being taught in the rue St Jacques. It has now almost ceased to function, and in the last analysis, probably its only enduring impact has been in the field of plainsong.

Nadia Boulanger always believed that musical roots lay firmly embedded in the past, and this conviction, in part, led her to propagate the music of Monteverdi. As she had written in January 1920:

'Our general knowledge, above all as far as musical history is concerned, is limited to a few dates and a few anecdotes – the latter more often than not destructive of illusion, since we fall over ourselves in discovering things that may diminish great people, much more than we force ourselves to explain their beauty for ourselves, to understand their apparent contradictions.'

Since then, of course, working musicians and, through them, the public at large, are much better informed, so what follows may not seem so compelling as it did fifty-six years ago:

'As for the works . . . a label gives us a modestly priced bet that carries no risk, and the name of the composer is the starting point for our judgement. Now, there is no evenness in production, but for discernment one needs independence of thought, relying on deep knowledge, on emotional sincerity and enthusiasm.

'The tyranny of technique in part blinds us, whilst analysis that is too anatomical makes us lukewarm. It is of course excellent if, over and above this analysis, there is an impassioned love of music and thought, an impassioned love of life and the ardent desire not to lose any of the beauty spread around us in indescribable profusion.'

Later in the same article she went on to analyse in more practical terms the reasons for the state of music in France at that time in respect of pre-Romantic composers, and the non-performance of certain works:

'The classics: some have disappeared. Is it a question of choirs? Evidently. All the same it is annoying that our country is the only one where the great oratorios are never performed, where Handel and Bach are in fact almost excluded . . . But Schubert, Brahms and the Bach suites! And so many more.'

As early as December 1919 she had deplored what she saw as the conventional attitude to the classics. But she maintained that it was simply an attitude, and not indicative of reality, for people either read them too soon or too quickly, without seeing what they truly represented in the history of music, of thought and of emotion. She maintained that it was not sufficient to have heard them, nor even to love them so as to appreciate their structure and beauty. Initiation had to be joined to revelation, so that one stood on 'the threshold of mystery'.

When she said this, she was not just harking back to the eighteenth century and earlier. She also had time and energy to deplore the fact that, owing to current attitudes, Mendelssohn was disappearing from the repertoire, and that he did not deserve such a fate. In England he also suffered a decline in favour among sophisticated people, though for others he never went out of fashion. Even so, it is only comparatively recently that his sheer technical skill has been fully recognized, and this has made him accepted once more by those who hesitated.

As we see, Nadia's musical tastes were broad, and she would constantly draw from her vast knowledge to illustrate a point or pursue a conversation. We find her at lunch with Paul Valéry and his wife in January 1939, discussing the Chopin Preludes with André Gide – and Gide congratulating himself on the fact that their views on the execution of the Preludes coincided. Not surprisingly Gide wanted to see more of Nadia Boulanger, but soon circumstances beyond even the determined Nadia's control were to come into operation, when it became obvious that World War Two was about to be launched. There were several reasons why she should have gone to America, but the decision to go there in wartime has been perhaps one of the few things that Nadia Boulanger has regretted. She never propounded any political beliefs, other than being intensely patriotic, by disposition a royalist, and in religion a Catholic, so one cannot accuse her of inconsistency on that score. One would be justified in thinking, however, that she might have elected to remain in France. Either way, it had little bearing on her career, except that going to America made it easier for her to be nearer Stravinsky, and to exercise her profession at a time when otherwise, in France, she would have been without pupils and without the necessary contacts for her work.

This natural break in her career is an appropriate point at which to consider Nadia Boulanger's views on musical education and development, which she had evolved over the years up to 1939 and have scarcely altered since then, and which she took with her to America.

4

The Teacher

Teaching is a vocation, and those who lack that vocation are very unwise to persevere once they become aware of the fact. It required no little courage for Nadia Boulanger to abandon all pretensions to a career as a composer, but she came to know that she could teach, and do it supremely well. This is why she is world famous. It may come as a surprise then to learn that she has no extraordinary or unusual teaching methods, nor has she perfected or elaborated any great theory of education. Her teaching is more by way of a philosophy of life, which she first lived out for herself, and then unfolded to her pupils.

Music, for her, must speak from the heart. The simplicity of this message may seem banal, but then the simplicity of it is deceptive. To speak from the heart implies first of all that the heart has something to say. For a composer, or for any artist concerned with communication, this is vital. As W. H. Auden has said, 'those who have no interest in communication do not become artists . . . they become mystics or madmen'. More fundamental still, to speak from the heart, an artist must know what his heart is saying, and that in turn implies that he must know his own self. And he takes the risk of learning that his whole career may prove in the long run to have been a search for his self.

Standing, as she did, on the threshold of a new century, and at the awakening of a whole new musical culture in the western hemisphere, there was obviously much that Nadia Boulanger could offer, particularly to musicians from a country such as America in the 1920s. She has compared it to Russia in the 1840s, full of inspiration but lacking training. She had behind her centuries of the European tradition, and the French branch of it in particular was especially well ordered. In her own character she combined Russian emotion with French precision and self-analysis – two extremely valuable influences.

Superficially it is easy to see why the French regard the Anglo-Saxons – as they are wont to call the British and Americans – as hypocrites. In the middle-class Anglo-Saxon tradition it was not considered the right thing to betray one's inner feelings. It followed from this that, in the eyes of Europeans, generations of such suppression often made the Anglo-Saxons unaware of their real feelings. Attitudes have changed in the second half of the twentieth century, but the tradition dies hard, and when a young person is still in search of those feelings, the quest for them may well appear to the French as hypocrisy, since they themselves rarely have to bother about them.

Possibly the greatest thing that one such Anglo-Saxon took away from four years of study in Paris was a saying of his music teacher: '*Il faut savoir ce qu'on veut.*' One must know what one wants, in all things, and if one cannot know what one wants, then one must know what one does *not* want, which is almost as good. So one begins to find the way to know oneself. When that has been achieved, the music will indeed speak from the heart. Of course the risks are enormous, and Nadia Boulanger is well aware of the fact. When a pupil is laying bare his inmost being, his whole musical life is at stake. Nadia Boulanger wants the pupil to be sure that what he has put down on paper, or how he interprets a particular passage, is what his own self really means, is what his own heart says.

There are times when a teacher has to be destructive to be constructive, and there is the terrible danger that he will stunt what might have been the individual's development, and impose in its place something of his own. By no means all musicians applaud Nadia Boulanger's methods and style. The critic and writer André Hodeir is possibly more noted for his attentions to jazz than to classical and serious music, but he has written:

'Now, once we agree that Hindemith's music is a lamentable error, we must go on to dismiss neoclassicism as a whole and, with it, nearly all of American music.

'For Piston, Thomson, and Copland have all been schooled in a tradition of decadent Stravinskyism, as taught by the musically short-sighted Nadia Boulanger, who enjoys considerable prestige in the United States and still exerts an unfortunate influence there.'

One cannot deny that Nadia Boulanger has been deeply influenced by Stravinsky throughout her career, but she never sought to impose any definite kind of style on her pupils. True, she can be strict in technical fields, but as Virgil Thomson has written: 'Her teaching of the musical techniques is . . . full of rigor, while her toleration of expressive and stylistic variety in composition is virtually infinite.'

Even those pupils who have developed along lines almost totally opposed to everything her tradition and background stand for marvel at the way that she has been able to come to terms with their music. It is here that her supreme technical equipment comes into its own. She is a faultless score reader, and can take virtually any piece of music and perceive its inner structure and development. Even in her seventies and eighties she has retained this ability, and is capable of sitting down at the piano and playing extremely difficult pieces from full score – and that despite terrible difficulties with her sight.

Her great gift is to draw out rather than impose, to guide rather than direct, which is surely the hallmark of mature teaching. It would be unrealistic to suppose that as an individual she is totally self-effacing, and of course there have been strong personality clashes with some would-be pupils. She has prejudices which, for a woman of her class and background, she finds impossible to abandon. She finds it hard to countenance over-familiarity, carelessness in dress, or lack of punctuality.

She has her musical prejudices, too, and of course for a teacher to impose dislikes is every bit as reprehensible as imposing personal preferences. Generally she tends not to mention the names of composers she does not like, rather than pronounce against them, but she has made little effort later in life to conceal the fact that she has little sympathy with the music of Rachmaninov, for example. When speaking of Idil Biret, the Turkish pianist, and one of her most brilliant recent pupils, she finds herself at a loss to explain why such a marvellous pianist is able to play such terrible music.

As it happens, Aaron Copland finds it hard to like Rachmaninov's music either: 'The prospect of having to sit through one of his extended symphonies or piano concertos tends, quite frankly, to depress me. All those notes, think I, and to what end? To me Rachmaninov's characteristic tone is one of self-pity and self-indulgence tinged with a definite melancholia.' He finds that as a fellow human being he has sympathy with a composer whose troubles inspire him to produce such music, but he feels that as a listener it is too much to take. Copland acknowledges Rachmaninov's sheer technical skill, and his ability to write beautiful long lines of melody but, as he points out, the techniques that Rachmaninov used were old-fashioned even in his own day, and when the melodic line is embroidered, the substance of the music itself becomes emptied of significance.

In this he is at one with Nadia Boulanger, who has always felt that the basic substance of music must be sound above any other consideration, and that no amount of addition, however attractive, can compensate for basic inadequacies.

One of the great tragedies of the second half of this century so far has been wavering uncertainty, with its concomitant liberalism – not informed, controlled or even necessarily compassionate liberalism, but destructive and aggressive liberalism in that it propagated the belief that any formalism was, by the very nature of things, bad. There are signs now that, after the hectic 1960s, when it seemed at times as if the whole of western civilization was sliding into the abyss, things have calmed down. In education it has once more become apparent that there were some things in the old system that simply could not be replaced. Often the signs have come from the young themselves. Even so, it may turn out to have been a very close-run thing.

There must have been many occasions when, particularly to the students on the barricades of Paris in 1968, for example, the whole world of Nadia Boulanger and all that it represented seemed a supreme irrelevance. Yet she survived, and the young are still sitting at her feet. Some soon find that they have to formulate a musical language of their own, and they soon outgrow what she has to teach them. They return to visit her, however, whenever they are able, they send her their compositions, and they write to her. She obviously holds something more for them than sentimental attachment to a beloved or revered teacher. She possesses a kind of charisma in their eyes. Above all she possesses innate taste. In the last analysis it is probably this that the people who know her would point to as her most precious gift.

The concept of taste is difficult to pin down. It cannot be taught, because it is intrinsic to each individual, and yet quite obviously some are able to acquire it. It is not directly communicable, because in the last resort it is entirely a matter for the individual. There are, however, obvious milestones along the road, and those who possess it are able to place those milestones for the benefit of others. They only serve to mark the way, however, and they cannot of their own accord bring us to the hoped-for destination. When asked what he most owed to Nadia Boulanger, the Swiss tenor Hugues Cuénod said that, after giving him the opportunity to sing in the first place, he most owed her that very thing, taste – taste in choice of programme and taste in the interpretation of the music itself. In *Le Monde Musical* for 15–30 January 1920, Nadia Boulanger wrote that her self-confessed aim – specifically in writing these articles, but it may as well be applied to her life's work – was as follows: 'My objective . . . is to arouse curiosity, to indicate the means of satisfying that curiosity, and to wish for the religion of music before and above the religion of the career. As for my personal opinion, it is of little importance.'

Already, then, she was working towards her concept of musical education, starting from the problem as she saw it:

'In listening to it [music] ought we to remain technicians, or ought we, released either from our profession or our knowledge, to find in music the stripping away of all the falsehoods that necessity, that education – frequently imperfectly understood – instill in us? It is easier to analyse a work in its form, in its evolution, than simply to love it with all the living forces of our heart. It is easier to define its peculiarities and its details than to draw out of it its emotion, its thought. In fact we do not always see in music all that is contained in it.'

A little further on she considers the contemporary state of music in France:

'Now, we all work very well at music. At the present time most musicians are able to use the practical terms which dissect and classify the different modes of its expression. But we do not have very much time – each one being specialized in one of its branches – to spend on music and, bending our fingers or our pen, we play or form notes, in unbelievable quantities, without really knowing what we are doing. We ought to take a step back so as to be able to understand it.

'Technically we know certain works from the past, no more than that, going towards the future without discernment, without the courage of judgement or the conviction that gives true admiration. The moment a work has a certain general movement, that it finishes in great strength or in restful smoothness, everything passes.'

At that time it would have been easy to attribute the malaise in French music to the disruptive effect of World War One, though, as Nadia Boulanger pointed out, it was all too easy to do so, since the war was unlikely to answer back, or even be worried by the charge. With characteristic candour, she went on: 'It is better to confess that virtually nothing happens for which we are not ourselves more or less directly responsible, and we should look for our part of the blame in each event.'

She went on to lament the choice of music offered in the current average concert in Paris, with the virtual exclusion of Bach, Handel, Schubert and Brahms, and the fact that contemporary works were usually only heard once, with the result that they could not be properly appreciated by, let alone become adequately known to, the musical world at large. She also made a plea for the young, for young composers and young foreign musicians:

'Ought not young foreign musicians and our own composers take their places alongside their elders? It is obvious that an intense amount of general evolution has taken place extremely quickly recently. Ought we not follow it, with moderation, naturally, but with sympathy? The English, with Bax, Holbrooke; the Belgians with Goossens and Jongen, the Spaniards with De Falla, the Russians with Scriabin and the Italians with Malipiero, and Casella, and certainly many more, are making an effort that we are not able to equate very well, but that we ought to know.'

As she pointed out, again with perfectly good sense, exchange is the best form of propaganda, and it was not right that French people, and musicians in particular, should artistically and intellectually despise the means that facilitated the expansion of science and industry. She felt that musicians should take full advantage of all the modern developments in the field of communication. She was too much of a realist, however, to imagine that national characteristics could be lost overnight, and indeed Nadia Boulanger would hardly want that, for she has always been intensely patriotic and appreciative of what each nationality had to offer: 'for if nature varies according to the climate, the human being undergoes the same process, and carries in himself the indelible characteristics of his race, his past and his history . . . Let us therefore welcome that which comes from beyond our frontiers, and let us in our turn spread the message of France – a great deal needs to be done on that score.'

As she revealed in a previous article (for December 1919), Nadia Boulanger was convinced that people had great difficulty, certainly in the France of those days, in combining intelligence and emotion, mind and pure sensation, reason and intuition. She felt that in art, and even more in the business of artistic education, this was a grave mistake, for the exclusion of the spontaneous faculties was just as wrong in her eyes as the exclusion of the cultivated faculties. In this she has always been lucky, because the dilemma for her has never existed – or at least if it did, she resolved it very early on in life.

She has always been a proponent of the *grande ligne*, both on a very practical and technical plane and on a more philosophical one. As an indication of the former, she wrote in December 1919:

'. . . the breaking up into fragments of the rhythm and the tune caused by the exaggerated importance given to the barline, by the multiplicity of nuances and by the tyranny of technique, create too many deep disturbances for the danger not to be pointed out.

'On the contrary, one only need set forward the broad planes, follow the linear development, underlining it with the harmonic or instrumental intentions, for the clarity to spread everywhere, and then everyone understands.'

She drew as her evidence for this conclusion the fact that the public is capable of suddenly giving an enthusiastic welcome to a work that they have not had time, reason or even the means to appreciate properly. Again, a work we are fond of may seem tedious on some days, or an unknown work boring, despite the fact that we know its principle and details to be interesting. Yet on other occasions we derive great satisfaction, and at times a collective enthusiasm, when we hear these same works.

Naturally a great deal depends on the conditions of the performance, and the creation of the tension between performers – and this includes the conductor, naturally – listeners, and the composer's music. But beyond that, it is the bringing out of the underlying movement, the great curve of line that is, to her, all-important. For some this may be too banal and too simple, but hard-bitten professional musicians, who have worked under her in her eighties, are enthusiastic about her approach to Fauré's *Requiem*, for example, and her insight into the work. Without ever dreaming of sacrificing one ounce of technical excellence, she sets out the *grande ligne*, and the music lives. In fact it lives because she has mastered all the technicalities and is left with the very soul of the music.

Although the theory of the *grande ligne* is, like so many theories, capable of abuse and of being misunderstood – or at worst being merely a cover for shallow musicianship when it should be exactly the opposite – it can be of great value to musicians. The rehearsals of the St John Passion with Menuhin for the Windsor Festival in 1970 were more in the nature of seminars, but when it came to the performance, the work moved from start to finish with an amazing coherence. This was surely the *grande ligne*. Again, from a very practical point of view, a musician often meets with a considerable problem of interpretation when performing pre-classical music that has been prepared in a modern performing edition with modern notation and barring, which has the effect of putting a strait-jacket on the music. One longs to be able to dispense with barlines altogether, so as to allow the musical phrases to take their natural course – once again the *grande ligne*.

From the listener's point of view the theory of the *grande ligne* raises the problem of the 'authentic' performance or interpretation. Assuming that the orchestra, or singers if it is a choral work, are carrying out the conductor's directions – and this is not always the case, of course – then presumably it should be possible to give a performance of a work that is as faithful to the composer's intentions as it is humanly possible to get. This ought, in theory, to render further recordings unnecessary, if the performance has been preserved on record or tape. This is manifestly not so, however, for orchestras have tonal variety as different as individual voices, or technique as different as individual solo instrumentalists. Moreover, listening to different recordings of the same work is always a fascinating and illuminating experience.

What, then, is the utility of Nadia Boulanger's advocacy of the *grande ligne*? Could there ever be a 'definitive' performance, in fact? In all fairness to her, the *grande ligne is* not claimed to guarantee the ultimate in performance, but is a key to release the soul of the music for performer and listener. Even when composers conduct their own works – assuming that they are all capable conductors, which they are not – there is no guarantee that their version will be the ultimate one. A brilliant new conductor may subsequently appear on the scene, or new tonal developments be made in certain instruments. In such circumstances a composer may well be only too happy to revise his ideas, or admit that a new version is 'better'. There again, all this is purely relative, since a performance, even when captured on record, is only one performance out of many, and each one is unique. No matter what a composer may hear in his inner ear as he writes down the notes and indicates the orchestral colour he conceives, at the moment of performance he can only speak through the performers.

In this respect music is possibly the most fragile and elusive of the communicating arts. A painter or sculptor has colour, shapes and volumes, which he can control fairly closely before he displays his work of art to the world and which are then in a permanent form, completely unaffected by nuances of interpretation. A writer has the printed word, yet even this begins to be elusive when people start to read his words aloud or, if he is a playwright, use them in conjunction with gestures and action on the stage. A musician, too, has language, but he is even less capable of ensuring that the exact interpretation is given to what he intends to convey, no matter how meticulously he may cover the score with indications of tempo, dynamic and expression.

When the composer is still living, the performers may appeal
to him for a reaction, and he may approve or criticize their
efforts. When a composer has only recently died, there are often
people alive who maintain that there is only one correct way to
perform a work, and that they are the faithful and only guard-
ians of that tradition – even when they are legion. When there
are no longer any such aids (or deterrents), one can only go
back to the available sources, such as the composer's own writings, what others wrote about his music, and what we can de-
termine of musical practice in his day. The further back in time
one goes, the more difficult this becomes, as we see from the
bitter controversy that has raged in recent years over ornamentation, or the orchestration of Monteverdi and Cavalli
operas. Then what may seem strange to ears in one century is
perfectly ordinary to ears in the next. J. S. Bach was already
old-fashioned by his sons' standards, and some of the instrumental effects that were novel to Berlioz' ears hardly seem to be
worth a mention today.

Binding everything together, however, are the facts that
music ultimately transcends all ages and all styles, and that it
has a fundamental appeal. Of course study will illuminate the
particular aspects of any one composer or school, and give us a
deeper understanding of the music, but one also needs a basic
musical sense, the *grande ligne*. Nadia Boulanger has always
sought to cultivate both these aspects. From the very earliest
days her teaching programme has included a study of the old
masters, for want of a better term, alongside the development of
those qualities she deems necessary, indeed essential, for real
musicianship. As she pointed out herself: 'It is rather curious to
note that once upon a time the most daring musicians, and
those most hostile to tradition from Beethoven to Schumann,
Berlioz to Wagner, cultivated the past.' As early as late 1919
she was regretting the fact that modern life was such a rush that
there was little time to go back over things, and that anything
dated, even if only from the day before, was outmoded. How
much more true that is in the second half of the century!

Youth has always had a tendency to be impatient with its immediate predecessors, whether it be Bach's sons calling him
old-fashioned or the young Nadia Boulanger telling her father
that the composers who were his idols were no good. To which

he replied: 'Perhaps you'll see one day that they weren't all that bad.' She has remembered that all her life, and it has probably made her relations with her pupils more tolerant as a result. She has always been able to hold a dialogue with the majority of her students, even when they were taken into domains of musical expression with which she felt little personal sympathy. For she has always professed that every epoch carried within itself its own modernism in relation to what had gone before. A study of its means of expression and general nature was not only useful for the light it shed on the music itself, but was also a good discipline – providing a basic education and foundation on which the young composer might build his own individual musical expression. Always, however, she enters the proviso that no matter what a student does, it must be done to the very best of his ability.

Although Nadia Boulanger nearly always makes her pupils go through the most elementary exercises, she would be the first to waive any particular part of the discipline if she thought that the pupil was sufficiently endowed in it. Indeed she has declined on occasion to take a pupil through a field in which she thought he was already quite competent, lest she hamper his natural development. While knowing precisely what she regarded as the ideal musical formation for students, she has nonetheless always tailored her teaching to individual needs. The goal has always been the same: to put into her pupils' hands the equipment necessary for making their particular contribution to music, and in the last analysis, by implication, to fulfil themselves.

As the Englishman Hugo Cole has written, recalling his time in Paris as a student with her in 1947:

'Nadia Boulanger was then sixty. Already her eyes were troubling her, so that she could hardly read a miniature score. But she had less need of scores than any other musician I have ever met. In her memory she seemed to hold all the music I have ever heard of and much that I hadn't. More remarkably still, she had the sort of memory she seemed to hold all the music I had ever heard of and latory passage, detail of scoring or figuration, that was needed to illuminate a teaching point. Bach's keyboard works and Beethoven's sonatas, needless to say, she knew like the back of her hand, but she would quote, too, Gounod's *Philémon et Baucis*,

Rameau and Monteverdi – then an almost unknown composer to most of us – or Weber's piano sonatas, for which she had great respect and admiration. She had an insight into the processes of her pupils' minds that enabled her always to keep one move ahead of the game; at a lesson, she would produce the score of a work, play it over, and discuss its structure. Later, you would realise that it was the work you had needed, at that moment, as a signpost to future progress.'

Yet as Virgil Thomson has pointed out, remarkable as her musicianship is, and devoted as she is to high standards, these two virtues are not her exclusive domain. What she does have, in Virgil Thomson's opinion, is critical acumen of a remarkable quality.

'She can understand at sight almost any piece of music, its meaning, its nature, its motivation, its unique existence; and she can reflect this back to the student like a mirror.

'Suddenly he sees that which has caused him pain, struggle and much uncertainty unveiled before him, without malice or invidious comparisons, as a being to which he has given birth. Naturally he is grateful. His work has been taken seriously, has received the supreme compliment of having its existence admitted to be real.

'Viewed in this warmly objective way, his piece may seem to him worth correcting or it may not. If its faults appear to be minor, eliminating them can be a joy. If this child seems born to be permanently a cripple, he may cherish it but not let it out into the world. Or he may let it die in a drawer and try to avoid the next time whatever has caused the hopeless deformity. All such decisions are up to him.'

Lennox Berkeley went even further, and said that he found it almost impossible to hand in a piece of music that was not up to standard. He felt an almost moral obligation, in response to this woman, to do his best. Even exercises had to be done with conviction. Indeed, without conviction there can, in Nadia Boulanger's estimation, be little, if any, worthwhile progress. This attitude stems not from any gloriously idealistic vision of the status of music and musicians, but from an innate feeling for humanity, since music is an expression of humanity itself. This hinges on the belief that once the pupil has learnt the necessary base, then her task as teacher is to draw out rather than to instill – to search for that which is natural or inherent, even, rather than create something artificial.

Some of Marcelle de Manziarly's earliest lessons had to be conducted by post because Nadia was in the South of France with her ailing sister Lili. The exercises were returned with such comments as 'The progression in bar ten is not particularly happy. Why not?' The implication was not that there was a simple choice between right and wrong, but that the pupil would, on reflection, automatically decide on what was best in the context and in that sense 'right'. Of course, told in this way, the process seems remarkably facile, but no amount of correction and repetition of exercises can instill something into a pupil if he does not understand why one thing is regarded as right and another wrong.

Virgil Thomson described the early lessons he attended in Paris in 1921:

'In her fourth-floor apartment at 36 Rue Ballu she gave, still gives, private lessons in all the chief musical branches – piano-playing, sight-reading, harmony, counterpoint, fugue, orchestration, analysis and composition.

'And there, of a Wednesday afternoon, took place weekly gatherings of pupils (strictly by invitation) at which the most modern scores of the time (by Stravinsky and Schönberg and Mahler) were analysed and played on the pianoforte, and the rarest madrigals of the Renaissance (by Monteverdi, Luca Marenzio and Gesualdo di Venosa) were sung in class. At the end of each session copious cakes were served and tea poured with frightening accuracy by the constantly trembling hand of Mademoiselle Boulanger's aged, rolypoly and jolly Russian mother, the Princess Mychetsky.'

The Wednesday afternoons changed eventually to become general analysis classes, attended by the majority of the pupils, after which Nadia Boulanger is at home to people who happen to be in Paris, or who come specially to see her from all over the world, and no one is excluded.

As to what actually happens at lessons, it depends on whether pupils attend individually or in a body. Virgil Thomson describes an individual lesson:

'The lessons take place with the teacher at the piano, the student in a chair at her right. She reads the score before her silently at first, then little by little begins to comment, spontaneously admiring here and there a detail of musical syntax or sound, expressing temporary reservations about another. Suddenly she will start playing (and perfectly, for she is a fabulous sight-reader) some passage that she needs to hear out loud or that she wishes the student to hear as illustration to her remarks.'

That was written in the early 1960s, when Nadia Boulanger was seventy-five. Writing of an earlier period, Hugo Cole said:

'Sometimes, you would be summoned for a lesson at 7 am; Mlle Boulanger had already been to Mass by then. If no pupil was to follow – and in 1947 the hectic pace of pre-war life had not yet been re-established – your lesson could last for two hours. I could never guess in advance what the next lesson would have in store for me. Sometimes the whole time would be spent on a single harmonic articulation. Sometimes you would progress (always from the music) to Rubens, Valéry, Kafka, cookery, or the importance of the swimming pool to the American way of life.'

This somewhat eclectic range of interests denotes two closely related things about Nadia Boulanger and her approach to teaching. The first is that she enjoys life and can relate that enjoyment to her work and communicate it to her pupils, often using striking images to illustrate the point she is making. As a recent young English student, Stephen Hicks, has said:

'She is a woman of tremendously wide culture, and she would bring this to bear on every aspect of music. She would always be very descriptive. She would give biblical texts throughout lessons, and these applied particularly in the Bach works. I'll never forget, for example, when studying with her the great G minor Fantasia and Fugue (BWV 542), a remark she would always make when you get to the chromatic passage in the middle. I think she used to call that the opening of the gates of hell or something like that. Anyway it was a marvellous image, and she would give such images frequently.'

The second thing is that, following on this tendency to relate elements from all aspects of her experience to her work, she relates all aspects of life to music, and vice versa. She would like all her students to be the sort of musicians who could think, hear and know everything, but also be capable of 'talking of nothing' at a dinner party, and of 'making the evening charming'. For her, knowledge without imagination is nothing. One is either bored to death with life or one is continually amazed by it. There must be a fire burning inside one, and there is little room in her life for dull, apathetic or boring people.

For her, life is fascinating, and so is her work. She expects her students to be of the same mind, and despite the amount of sheer technical matter to be dealt with, she can never divorce music from life. Both must be lived passionately, for music relates to life in a very close way. Yehudi Menuhin describes it as seeing all life as a unity, a monumental pillar, which he attributes to a quality of mysticism that comes from her half-Russian parentage. Music, as an integral part of the pillar, is part of life. As she herself has said: 'The art of music is so deep and profound that to approach it very seriously *only*, is not enough. One must approach music with a serious rigour and, at the same time, with a great, affectionate joy.'

This is why she is capable of being hard, even cruel, to students who take their work lightly or who fail to commit themselves to it. This is why she has little time for students who frequently arrive late or tired, or who are unduly nervous or timid. For one thing she knows full well how demanding the career of a professional musician is, and therefore how vital sleep and an adequate diet are, but she also feels very strongly that if one chooses to do something by the exercise of the free will, then one must do it very well.

In many respects her maternal instincts were reserved for generations of students, many of whom she cared for as if they were her own children, and some of whom she scolded like any mother who cared for their safety and well-being. Obviously this did not suit all her pupils, and some went their own way with regret, yet paying tribute to the qualities of the woman. A few felt that they had been treated badly, even provoked into going, but if that be so, it may well have been her way of acknowledging that in such cases she had nothing to offer. Out of the hundreds and hundreds of students it is perhaps remarkable that there are so few 'casualties'.

She has been proud to have been the teacher of so many and such gifted pupils. As she said recently: 'I love to teach, I love to be with the students. I feel it a very great privilege, and I think that I can help them to go through stages of development which are arduous, and difficult, and encourage them – in a way impose a certain law, a certain habit of "doing one's daily duty".'

It is this attitude which inspired Virgil Thomson to describe her as 'a one-woman musical UN', and as musical America's Alma Mater; and on sheer weight of numbers alone, she has probably given more to America than to any other country. It is a country for which she has a deep affection, which was founded over fifty years ago, strengthened during the years before and during World War Two, and still remains undiminished today.

For all her insistence upon the traditional disciplines, however, the really efficacious teaching occurs at the point of contact with the pupil. It is something akin to an electric current that is capable of flowing both ways: from teacher to pupil and vice versa. It does not happen automatically, nor indeed during every lesson. Nor will it be the same with every pupil, let alone during every lesson with the same pupil. Each occasion is a totally individual experience. Sometimes the lesson will be fruitful, but fairly routine, while on other occasions pupil and teacher experience something quite extraordinary, which leaves them both feeling exhilarated, and later the pupil probably exhausted. This is what gives teachers generally the courage to persevere and pupils the desire to return time and time again. It may happen only rarely, but when it does, it is ample reward for hours of the humdrum. None of this is the exclusive domain of Nadia Boulanger, except that she is indefatigable, and possibly she makes it happen much more often than anyone else, and for a remarkably wide variety of pupils. Also, if the electric current connects, then what the pupil gains is probably much more highly concentrated than almost anywhere else. This is why she is a unique teacher.

The connection might begin with only the merest flicker, but she is capable of turning it into a pyrotechnic display. She will first read or play a composition through, or, if it is a question of a performer interpreting a work for voice or instrument, she may well accompany him herself, hearing the piece through from beginning to end, probably without any sort of comment, but listening, thinking, comparing all the time. She will then go back to the beginning, but this time get only a number of bars into the piece before she starts a third time; here probably only the first phrase will be taken, and then, after a brief pause, she will begin to deliver the apposite observations she has stored up mentally in the few minutes that have just elapsed.

Now all her remarkable musical knowledge will be deployed in a seemingly inexhaustible torrent. The smallest detail of the music will be examined for the student, and its importance in relation to the whole composition pointed out for him, thus achieving complete clarity. If he is a performer, and unable to cope with a particular passage, she will devise some imaginative kind of exercise there and then, quite spontaneously, so as to help him master the difficulty. If she is giving a master class, she will somehow manage to bring all those present directly into what is going on, even if they are not called upon to demonstrate in person.

Then at the other end of the scale, the work will be related to its antecedents and put within its historical, and even social, context. From her vast stores of knowledge she will quote examples, like a juggler who keeps producing ever more and more objects, throwing them up into the air, and keeping them there in glittering profusion before the audience's eyes. What had formerly been isolated fragments are now codified into a seemingly fantastic order. Teacher and pupils are swept along in the excitement of discovering together the infinite riches that music has to offer.

There, at the centre, burning with a 'hard, gemlike flame', and maintaining the ecstasy – though she would probably not have approved of Pater's application of the image in its context – is Nadia Boulanger. Her energy seems inextinguishable, her presence electrifying. The student is confronted by a frail woman who is at the same time larger than life. Her gestures, her way of talking, her figures of speech, her far-ranging sources of reference, all leave a lasting impression. She is capable of praising, cajoling, criticizing, or even badgering, at a second's notice, yet not a moment of this virtuoso performance is gratuitous. Indeed, its only *raison d'être* is the inspiration and information of the pupil, and the point of departure is always a specific problem and a desire to help the pupil eliminate it. Each lesson, each piece of music, is a voyage of discovery that may take the pupil to shores he had never dreamed existed. It may also lead him into something akin to the valley of the shadow of death. The ultimate destination may not turn out to be the House of the Lord, but with Nadia Boulanger as his guide, it will certainly have brought him face to face with genius, and probably with himself. It is a voyage that she made for herself at the outset of her career, and from which she returned with the almost superhuman stature that has enabled her to sustain her position for so long, and made such an impression on generations of pupils.

To those who are aware, who connect, there is always something to be learnt, even from an ostensibly inferior performance, since the listener is inspired by it to reflect on what would have improved that performance, and so come closer to understanding the performer's technical problems and the work itself. It may not necessarily be pleasant, or even comfortable, to listen to such a performance, and there is no virtue in attempting here to justify inferior performances as an end in themselves. It is, moreover, in the nature of things that a performer will almost inevitably wish that certain points in his rendition had been different. If there were no incentive to improve, the implications for music – or for that matter any art – would indeed be serious.

It has been Nadia Boulanger's particular attribute that she has almost always been able to draw out of her pupils, and lead them on to, performances that in their wildest dreams they had never imagined themselves capable of. In a certain sense they go beyond themselves, and the two interdependent factors that produce this are her inspiration and her very presence, manifested through her rigour and her enthusiasm. She is a catalyst, and here one must add that the process has not always led to a student fulfilling his ambitions in the way he had envisaged. Self-knowledge can be a source of great strength, but it can also work the other way. To this she replies that if one chooses to do something, one must do it supremely well. Apart from any other considerations, the musical profession is usually a difficult one to pursue with success, and she would be failing in her duty to her students if she allowed them to think otherwise.

Over and above this, however, is her vision of the role of music in relation to life, which lays down that one is morally bound to aim only for the best. Her students are led to understand this, and respond accordingly. They simply feel that they must do their best for her, and the very fact that she takes them seriously generally makes them work harder than they ever worked before. Even she cannot make a silk purse out of a sow's ear, however, and for every success there are as many who sink without trace. Almost any teacher would like all his students to be successful, not primarily to boost his own reputation, but more for the pupil's sake. Even if they do not become consummate musicians, almost all Nadia Boulanger's pupils carry away a vivid and lasting impression, which will remain with them for the rest of their lives. It may be that listening to a certain piece of music recalls her analysis of it for them; it may only be the memory of one of her many aphorisms, her vivid metaphors, or simply her voice; whatever it is, in the last resort it is her personality, or any combination of some aspects of it. Herein lies her unique quality, which no one can reproduce, or explain adequately, to those who have never experienced it at first hand, since it elicits an individual response in each person. Happily some indication of her art has been preserved on film made for television, but it is rather like having the whole of Greek sculpture represented in a museum by one incomplete statue. The fruits of her work now stretch right round the world, however, and she will go on teaching for as long as she is able.

5

World War Two and Since

Some Europeans found themselves in America when war broke out in 1939, and others went there soon after. Stravinsky had been asked by Harvard University to give a course in the poetics of music in 1939, so when war broke out he decided to stay in America, and subsequently went to live in California. Ironically enough, Schönberg was almost a neighbour, but the two men were destined never to meet. There were some odd products of this war period among Stravinsky's compositions, such as the Polka for an elephant in Barnum's circus in 1942, the ballet music for Billy Rose two years later, and the Ebony Concerto of 1945 for Woody Hermann and his Boys. Alongside these, however, was a series of more substantial works, such as the Symphony in Three Movements (1945), and in the immediate postwar period the ballet *Orpheus* (1947) and the Mass (1948).

Nadia spent almost the entire time she was in America with Winifred Hope Johnstone and her sister in Boston, at their house on Bay State Road, apart from a few months in California so as to be near Stravinsky. Miss Johnstone was secretary of the Lili Boulanger Memorial Fund, and had been since it was founded in 1939 from the proceeds of a benefit concert given on 6 March that year in Symphony Hall, Boston. On that occasion Nadia directed members of the Boston Symphony Orchestra, the Harvard Glee Club and the Radcliffe Choral Society in a programme of works by Bach, Beethoven, Malipiero and Lili Boulanger.

The aims of the Fund are twofold: to keep alive the memory and the music of Lili, and to aid composers of exceptional talent and integrity by an annual award. Alexei Haieff was the first recipient, in 1942, and since then the list of successors has remained distinguished and become international. Americans have included Robert Crane, Paul DesMarais (twice), Ned Rorem, Noël Lee, Easley Blackwood, Charles Wuorinen (twice), Paul Seiko Chihara, Robert Levin (twice), Yung Shen, Hugh Robertson and James S. Harrison. As one might expect, Poland has had several recipients, namely Michal Spisak, Antoni Szalowski (twice), Wojciech Kilar and Zygmunt Mycielski. Two other Iron Curtain countries to receive awards have been Czechoslovakia and Romania, with Karel Husa and Alexandru Hrisanide respectively. Latin America is represented by Claudio Spies from Chile, Claudio Santoro from Brazil, and Jose Almeida Prado, also from Brazil, who won the award both in 1972 and 1973. Only two women have received the award – the British composer Thea Musgrave, and the Turkish pianist Idil Biret – and only three Frenchmen – Jean-Michel Dufay, Bruno Gillet and Léo Préger (twice). The list is completed by three Englishmen in Nicholas Maw, Edwin Roxburgh and Christopher Bochmann; the Italian Gianpaolo Brocali; the Dane Per Norgaard; and the Indian Varaj Bhatia.

As to Nadia herself, we find her on 26 October 1941 giving a concert in the Boston Museum of Fine Art, with a programme of early French music, along with works by Debussy, Poulenc, Ravel and Fauré. On 7 May 1942 she was at Madison Avenue, New York, with a similar mixture for the Co-ordinating Council of French Relief Societies. On 24 May she was in Boston where she accompanied Doda Conrad in Schubert's *Schöne Müllerin*. Marcelle de Manziarly afterwards asked the two performers to autograph her programme, and characteristically Nadia Boulanger wrote: 'What a strange idea! But then . . . for Mar(celle) Nadia B.' Two days later we find her at the Longy School of Music, Cambridge, and so she progressed around America, giving lectures and recitals and lessons, but based most of the time on Boston.

Nadia Boulanger was happy to be at Harvard University for the festival organized for the 100th anniversary of the birth of Fauré from 27–30 November 1945 inclusive, and she performed there herself on 2 December that year. She has given much to America over the years, especially in its earlier need for encouragement and stimulation of its musical life, but her roots have always been in France, and in Paris in particular; and, like all Parisians, she was happy to be able to return after the war, even if it was to a ravaged country. Paris itself had escaped physical destruction, but it obviously took some time for the life of the city, and that of Nadia Boulanger, to resume its prewar rhythm.

Leaving America meant leaving the possibility of contact with many of the brilliant musicians who had gone there at the outbreak of war, including Bartók, Martinu, Milhaud, Nabokov, Artur Schnabel, Stefan Wolpe, and Lukas Foss. She was not alone, however, in feeling that her roots lay in the country of her birth. Benjamin Britten also went to America at the outbreak of war, but quickly realized that he would only be happy where his roots had been, in his native county of Suffolk.

What was perhaps sad was that postwar Paris was no longer the focus of artistic and cultural activity that it had been in the Twenties and Thirties, though it took a long time for people to realize the fact. For the teaching of music, however, the environment is much less important than the teacher, and what Nadia Boulanger offered her pupils did not depend on the number of concerts given in any one season in Paris, or the composers working there.

Obviously it helps enormously if there are other things, too, but for students to come to Paris and see life in this or any such city is in itself a very beneficial experience at that point in their development. It is certainly so for Europeans, and presumably is even more beneficial for Americans, who might otherwise never come into contact with the wellsprings of Western culture.

Nadia Boulanger naturally regretted one particular postwar gap, for in 1945 Stravinsky decided to abandon French nationality and take up American; and it seemed as if he had turned his back on Europe completely, until it was decided that the première of *The Rake's Progress* should take place in Venice in 1951. This was yet another turning point in his career, since it marked the end of his 'musical model' approach to composition, and brought him back into contact with the developments that had taken place in postwar European music – most importantly, dodecaphonic serial music, and that of Webern in particular. In the view of René Leibowitz,

Webern's importance lay in the fact that he related Schönberg's discoveries to the future, whereas Berg related them to the past.

This spectacular *volte-face* on Stravinsky's part placed Nadia Boulanger in a considerable predicament. Indeed, her progressive isolation – in France especially, but to some extent from the international avant-garde mainstream also in later years – has been attributed to this failure to embrace new developments in the field of dodecaphony and serial music. For so much of his career until 1951 Stravinsky was the living example of all that Nadia Boulanger looked for in a composer and held up to her students. He had accepted the past as an essential part of his musical make-up, and yet worked in the present.

As one might expect, however, from a person of Stravinsky's genius, he did not swallow dodecaphony and all that went with it lock, stock and barrel. He handled it in exactly the way his temperament dictated, so that he once more became the original creator, taking existing elements, expressing himself through them, and producing works of art in their own right. Naturally this became apparent in the music, and eventually Nadia Boulanger was able to assure herself that he had not gone against everything they had originally stood for.

By way of analogy, a quotation from something said about a previous situation is apposite to the one here. Writing in *Chroniques de ma vie* about Rimsky-Korsakov's attitude to Debussy, Stravinsky had this to say:

> 'But I must do justice to Rimsky-Korsakov, and to Liadov too, for in spite of their disapproval they had enough courage and sensitiveness not to condemn wholesale all the serious and valuable things modern art had to offer. Here is a specimen that characterizes the older master's attitude towards Debussy. At a concert where one of the latter's works was in the programme I asked Rimsky-Korsakov what he thought of it. He replied in so many words: "Better not listen to it; you risk getting used to it, and then you would end by liking it."'

By comparison with what had gone before Debussy, and the new tendencies he represented, the implications of serial music were much more serious. Apart from the fact that she felt it would divide the musical world – which it virtually has, and in this she was very perspicacious – Nadia Boulanger was against it because, when taken to its logical conclusion, it dehumanizes music. She is by no means blindly opposed to it, for she is perfectly capable of seeing its good points, and appreciating it from a purely technical point of view. She can even discuss it with students almost as an exercise. More than that, however, it would be unreasonable to expect, since it strikes at the root of all she holds sacred.

Naturally one can argue that a 'good' teacher should be able to embrace all the necessary equipment for a pupil about to embark on a career. In this context one of the few specific criticisms of Nadia Boulanger concerns her attitude to dodecaphony. As Virgil Thomson has written:

> 'She does not, however, encourage her students in twelve-tone-row composition, which she considers to be a form of musical "speculation" in the philosophical sense of the word, rather than a road to expression. She has found that Stravinsky, whose "genius" has already protected him through many another perilous adventure, experimenting with it in his seventies is not reproachable. Nor can she find it in her heart to blame the young Pierre Boulez for far-outness, considering the phenomenal brilliancy of his mind and the impeccable nature of his musical ear. She does believe, however, that serial dodecaphony is in general a musical heresy and that its influence risks creating as permanent a division among musicians in the West as the Protestant Reformation did among Christians.
>
> 'All this, the musical Left might easily answer, is also speculation. And if the young need lessons in traditional music making, as Boulez himself admits, then these can be accepted from any competent musician, even from Nadia Boulanger.'

Of course Thomson was writing in 1962, and since then – almost incredibly, it seems – Nadia Boulanger has to a certain extent come to terms with dodecaphony in her students' compositions. Some have said that Stravinsky more or less obliged her to take to it when he did so himself, hence Virgil Thomson's slightly equivocal reference above. Though Nadia Boulanger has rarely indicated her feelings about individual composers, she wrote about Schönberg as long ago as January 1947 in a review for *Le Spectateur* of a performance of the Piano Concerto at the Salle Gaveau in Paris. In it she set out her attitude to this kind of music.

She had been particularly impressed by the amount of young people attending the concert. This led her to ask the question 'why?' As a statement of her position she began by saying that she was not questioning the worth of Schönberg, since that was undeniable, but she professed herself scarcely able to believe that young people could still, in those days, be under the domination of what she called his 'tormented and romantic art'. Her objections were that the young were unlikely to find a path in a system that was unable to conceive, and even positively outlawed, relaxation in the music, and whose only basis was the most complicated sonorities.

She asked whether the young adopted the system out of conviction or anxiety. Were they making a rather desperate attempt because they lacked direction? She had heard one of the most gifted saying that it was an 'experiment' that they ought to make, which would obviously conflict with her theories of musical education, and indeed with her concept of the very nature of music itself. Or were they sure of having found their way, and were therefore ready for all the sacrifices and renunciations implicit in such a musical discipline?

She then went on to state her position – within the limits one might expect of her – and the basic reservation she put forward was that the music of Schönberg was, despite its mastery, enigmatic and inhuman. The means used to achieve its effect were, in her eyes, so complex that it was difficult to appreciate them all while listening to the music, and if one so competent as herself found it difficult – this by implication – then the problem must have been all the more acute for less gifted listeners. She also felt that everything was sacrificed to intellectual research, and that so much effort in search of an emotion that did not spring from itself was sterile. She deplored the lack of any perceptible interior joy, and while wishing that it were otherwise, concluded that despite such an astonishing array of technical discoveries, such confident writing and such total lucidity, the end result was a kind of negation. Despite this rejection of Schönberg's music, she was manifestly appreciative of the piano playing of Yvonne Loriod – then a relative newcomer, and not yet so exclusively associated with Olivier Messiaen and his music.

Be that as it may, this reaction alone would not even begin to satisfy many musicians whose tendencies are by no means exclusively towards the avant-garde but who feel that Schönberg simply cannot be dismissed in so final a way. In defence of Nadia Boulanger we have Virgil Thomson's testimony that she was analysing Schönberg's music for him as a student in the Twenties; and that of the distinguished French conductor Georges Tzipine, who said that it was virtually Nadia Boulanger on her own who introduced Bartók to the French musical world, and was using Honegger's music as material for her analysis classes in the Twenties. And Yehudi Menuhin has said that she knows Berg's *Wozzeck* extremely well.

Not surprisingly, she had more to say about it herself, and in *Le Spectateur* of February 1947 she went further with her examination of the problem of contemporary music. She began by saying that the public was automatically blamed, for not liking music at all, or for being afraid of modern music, or for being stuck in its old grooves. She agreed that the public had been notoriously wrong on several occasions in its treatment of certain works, that it was slow to tune in to new developments, as well as being rather lazy and even mean over acquiring anything musically new. She also deplored the average level of culture.

However, she laid the major part of the blame on the musicians themselves, or more specifically on those responsible for the devising of programmes. The public was expected to take part in new ventures, and was drowned in mediocrity. Good and bad were offered indiscriminately, and then the people who chose the programmes expressed surprise, saying that it was the public which lacked discernment, only giving a coldly polite welcome to experiments that amused no one.

She maintained that it was obvious that when the public was offered the choice between good music and better music, it infallibly went for the better music. When offered good and worse music, it went for the worse; and when a hotch-potch was served up, including the mediocre, then the public was lost. In other words, it was extremely difficult to excuse any concession to the mediocre in the choice of programmes. In her estimation these concessions revealed more often than not an uncertainty and a negligence rather than a mere expediency.

Whether one excused, understood or condemned, however,

this did not modify the consequences and the effect on the public. In such circumstances it was deplorable that the public did not get angry. There was no good in pointing to the fact that the people responsible were cynical, saying that the public by and large did not care, and asking what sort of protest would be made in any case. If only there were some who were aware – and such people did in fact exist – then they mattered, and had to be taken into consideration.

In this context she particularly praised the initiative in France of the Jeunesses Musicales in their work to educate the public. As she pointed out, it was no good simply being enchanted by music without understanding the quality of it. This was merely an illusion. In any case, an artist got no real satisfaction from convincing an audience that was already disposed to absorb anything and everything, nor the listener in absorbing everything without the chance to choose.

If taken to its logical conclusion, this argument might eventually lead one to assume that the composer was necessarily tributary to the listener. Nadia denied this, however, because for her the composer's creative urge was a necessity coming to fruition in his composition. The completed work only had any effect, however, if those listening were capable of appreciating it. All turned then, in her opinion, on that precise moment at which the work and the listener met, and on their respective inner qualities. On the part of the listener this obviously calls for a certain willingness to educate himself so as to be able to approach the work, on its own terms as far as possible, so as to give it a fair chance at the hearing and, if possible and if necessary, listen to it again. Nadia Boulanger always deplored the fact that there was so little opportunity to hear new works more than once (if at all) in the Paris of the inter-war years.

From the performer's point of view this also had implicit demands. As she said in another context about interpretation generally: 'You must play in such a way that the audience quite naturally feels intelligent.' So each concert is, by implication, a unique occasion, when the three elements of composer, performer (which here includes any conductor) and listener combine in a simultaneous act of creation. Obviously the conductor's role is here of paramount importance, and yet could not exist without the other performers or the composer.

The postwar period saw Nadia Boulanger re-establishing herself in Paris as a teacher of international status, and attracting students again from all over the world. At first they came particularly from England, since it was near, and from America. Of those who came from across the Channel in the years between the wars, Lennox Berkeley is possibly the most distinguished pupil Nadia Boulanger has had, and he was one of the first. Not long later, Peggy Glanville Hicks came all the way from Australia. Some of the more recent from England have been Edwin Roxburgh, Nicholas Maw, David Wilde and Stephen Hicks. One of the few distinguished women composers to emerge in England in recent years, Thea Musgrave, also studied with Nadia Boulanger. After the first wave of American pupils in the early Twenties, there had been a second wave which included Robert Russell Bennett, Arthur Berger, Marc Blitzstein, Paul Bowles, Israel Citkowitz, David Diamond, Irving Fine, Ross Lee Finney, Alexei Haieff, John Lessard, Harold Shapero, Elie Siegmeister, Howard Swanson, Louise Talma and John Vincent. They in turn had generated interest in her, and sent pupils to her.

It would be foolish to pretend that everyone who went to study in Paris with Nadia Boulanger came back uttering her praises. This will be looked at in closer detail later in this book, but despite these examples, pupils continued to flock to the rue Ballu and to Fontainebleau. Yet there have always been remarkably few from her native France. Igor Markevitch was promising, but abandoned composition, and the work of Jean Françaix is admitted as being elegant and amusing, but not perhaps particularly heavyweight in the musical league. Some people find his music simply vulgar. He is, however, himself in his music, without reservation, and is quite content to be no more or less than that. In Nadia Boulanger's canon he has fulfilled himself. As she said in 1946 in relation to his suite *La Douce France*: 'With the certitude of those who know that they want, Jean Françaix goes on his way without being bothered by good advice. He is himself and does not look for any other.' Three years later she conducted the first performance, which was broadcast by the BBC in London, of his Symphony for string orchestra.

Nadia Boulanger's lack of French pupils has often been the

subject of debate, some of it malicious. Obviously in her work at the Conservatoire and the Ecole Normale she had several French pupils, and some of them were quite gifted. Having been discovered by Americans, and other nationalities from all over the world, it is not surprising that on a purely proportionate basis she should have had fewer French students of note. She has never been a forcing school for genius. As she said in 1973: 'You can only actually give the student the means to express himself. You cannot change what he is, but you can help him to discover who he is. But you will never make him more than he is. That is why I consider that the teacher can do only very little, honestly speaking.'

She has been charged with only taking good students, but Yehudi Menuhin for one hotly denies this, and maintains that she does take the less gifted students. The American composer Roy Harris, who studied with her some fifty years ago, put on record an account of how Nadia Boulanger chose those whom she decided to accept as students, and this slightly humorous conversation may well have contributed to the charge of selectivity. Moreover fifty years ago she was relatively much less in demand than she was even forty years ago. As Harris said:

'Nadia Boulanger told me this way she has of deciding who to accept for students. Those who have no talent, and those who have no money; these are not acceptable. There are those who have talent but no money. These she accepts. Those who have little talent but much money she also accepts. But those who have much talent and much money she says she never gets.'

The Englishman Hugo Cole, who went to her in 1947, confirms the evidence of her generosity, since for the whole of his first year's lessons Nadia Boulanger refused to take any payment, though later he brought from England a set of Bartók's *Mikrokosmos* for her, as a gift. These had been completed in 1937, but were not easy to obtain in postwar France. This again shows how up to date she has always managed to be, despite even the upheaval of a war.

What is a much more just estimation of Nadia Boulanger's criteria for selection of students turns on her evaluation of a potential student's character. When asked about this, she answered:

'. . . bad character is rather nice and interesting. But when you have no character, no inner quality, I mean when somebody has no inner energy, has no inner enthusiasm, is unaware, is unpresent, what can you do? You can do nothing. Somebody who is wrong, who is wild, who is badly brought up, who is savage, you can help him. He has an inner energy, he has an inner strength, and that you cannot give him, nor can you take away. But you can help him to have the other, which will bring logic, a construction, in all that he is.'

Such criteria cut right across nationality.

Here is Hugo Cole describing his experiences in those early years after World War Two: 'I arrived in Paris in the spring of 1947 with £60 in travellers' cheques wrung from a grudging Treasury and a suitcase full of tins of corned beef – basic supplies for six months to be spent studying with Nadia Boulanger.' He was very lucky in finding somewhere to live more or less straight away in the apartment of a French music publisher's widow. Although the accommodation left much to be desired, there was a good Pleyel grand piano that had always been kept in tune. Hugo Cole discovered subsequently that his landlady was also a great Anglophile, and that every day of the war she had stationed herself in front of a photograph of King George VI and drunk a toast to an English victory. They rarely met, but he would sometimes see her on Sundays, beautifully made up, walking slowly and alone down the Champs-Elysées.

At this time, late 1946 and early 1947, Nadia Boulanger was writing music criticism for *Le Spectateur*: noting with pleasure performances of works by her pupil Jean Françaix and her beloved Stravinsky, musing on the phenomenon of Schönberg, expressing regret at the death of talented colleagues, and uttering reproof where she deemed this necessary.

She also gave a series of concerts at the Union Interalliée in Paris. On 14 January 1947 she played two-piano music by Stravinsky with Jean Françaix, and accompanied the baritone Gérard Souzay in Schubert. In March of that year there was an *In Memoriam* programme for Lili Boulanger, and in April an all Monteverdi programme. In December 1948 there was a programme devoted to Bach, and in January 1949 the American pianist Noël Lee performed. In 1953 he received the Lili Boulanger Memorial Fund award for that year. In 1949 Nadia Boulanger became Director of the American Conservatory at

Fontainebleau, a post she still jealously holds more than twenty-five years later, and after more than fifty years of teaching there.

On 2 December 1950 Dinu Lipatti died. His life had been short – he was born on 19 March 1917 – but his career brilliant. On 9 January 1951 Nadia presided over a programme entitled 'Homage to Dinu Lipatti', and during the course of the evening records of his were played.

It was lucky for posterity that something of Dinu Lipatti's mastery was preserved on record, and it was lucky also that Nadia Boulanger was making records in the early 1950s. These were on the Decca Gold Label series, and included French vocal music of the Renaissance by such composers as Josquin des Prés, Clément Jannequin, Claude Lejeune, Orlando de Lassus, Guillaume Costeley, Claudin de Sermisy, Jacques Maudit and Pierre Bonnet. There were also extracts from operas by Marc-Antoine Charpentier and Jean-Philippe Rameau, and a further selection of vocal and instrumental works by Monteverdi.

March 1952 was the occasion for another Lili memorial concert. Nadia had always wanted to record Lili's music, and six years later she saw the realization of this most cherished project. Igor Markevitch, who had probably been the most gifted of her pupils from the Franco-Russian group of the late Twenties, was the conductor on whom the task finally devolved. The record contains three settings of Psalms – 24, 129 and 130 (which is dedicated to the memory of Ernest Boulanger) – *Vieille prière bouddhique* and *Pie Jésus*, Lili's last work, which she dictated line by line when she was no longer able to write. Markevitch now has Italian nationality, but he has maintained strong ties with France. From 1957 to 1961 he was conductor of the Concerts Lamoureux, and in 1968 became conductor of the Monte Carlo Opera Orchestra. After an initial period as a composer of promise, his fame now rests more on his conducting ability.

In 1956 Nadia attended the festival of contemporary music in Warsaw. Of all countries, after America and England, Poland has been especially of interest to her. She proudly lists the order of Polonia Restituta among the honours awarded her, and Tadenz Szeligowski, Kazimerz Serocki, Grazyna Baciewicz, Antoni Szalowski, Wojciech Kilar, Zygmunt Mycielski and

Michal Spisak are some of the more distinguished Polish musicians with whom she has been associated. No doubt she
would like to have had much more to do with music in the countries of the Communist bloc if the occasion had presented itself.

For Nadia's seventieth birthday in 1957 Jean Françaix wrote
a cantata entitled *Komm meine heilige Nadia*, doubtless with apo-
logies to J. S. Bach. In 1962 she went to the Gstaad Festival with
the Menuhins, and also conducted the New York Philharmonic
in New York in Fauré's *Requiem*, Virgil Thomson's *A Solemn
Music*, and Lili's setting of Psalm 130, *Du fond de l'abîme*. This
was in fact a series of four concerts, beginning on 15 February,
and Nadia was in her seventy-fifth year. Virgil Thomson wrote
an article for the occasion in which he described her as a person
who 'for more than forty years has been, for musical Americans, a one-woman graduate school so powerful and so per-
meating that legend credits every US town with two things – a
five-and-dime and a Boulanger pupil.'

The year 1967 was obviously important in Nadia
Boulanger's life, with the approach of her eightieth birthday.
The highlight of the celebrations was a gala concert and recep-
tion on the birthday itself, organized by Doda Conrad and a
group of close friends at the opera house in Monte Carlo, in the
presence of Prince Rainier III and Princess Grace. Nadia
Boulanger's connections with Monaco were formed with
Prince Rainier's father, and she is Maître de Chapelle to the
Grimaldi family, in which capacity she was responsible for the
music at Prince Rainier's marriage in 1956.

Among the distinguished artists and musicians taking part in
the birthday gala were Marc Chagall, Igor Markevitch, Louise
de Vilmorin, Yehudi Menuhin, Jean Françaix, and the poet St
John Perse, who wrote the following tribute:

'Nadia, the centuries change their visage and their tongue, but
Music, your century, has no masks to strip away since, more than
any art and any science of language, it is the knowledge of the Being.

'To you, Nadia, free and yet a vassal of the great musical family,
but a subject of this divinity alone, which knows no territory, no
school and no rite.

'To the person who, in America, in the darkest hours of the western drama, I saw living out amongst us her life as an apostle and
sibyl – animating, instigating, educating and liberating; her ear at

77

every source and her spirit alive to every current, a leaf fluttering in the immense foliage – 'to her be honour and thanks, in the name of Music itself.'

It was also at this gala that Prince Rainier invested her with the insignia of a Commander of the French Legion of Honour.

The following year saw an exhibition at the Bibliothèque Nationale in Paris, when some 130 or so items were gathered together to commemorate the fiftieth anniversary of the death of Lili, and shortly afterwards Nadia achieved another of her aims when she persuaded the municipality of Paris to name the intersection of the rue Ballu on to which her apartment looks the Place Lili Boulanger. In 1971 there was yet another fiftieth anniversary, this time of the founding of the American Conservatory at Fontainebleau, and as usual she threw herself into the planning of the event with the enthusiasm and energy of a person half her age.

So she continues, travelling less now, but finding time to be a regular visitor to the Yehudi Menuhin School in England, and the Royal College of Music in London. She adjudicated at the most recent Leeds international piano competition, conducted her beloved Fauré *Requiem* for the BBC, and gave master classes on television, surviving tiring sessions on pots of yogurt in the breaks and then returning refreshed to the fray.

Anyone may go to her Wednesday afternoons, either to the analysis classes or, when the students have departed, for the conversation afterwards. Nadia takes her place near the piano, and a game of musical chairs without the music ensues. A random survey of those present might find one of Stravinsky's sons; the Polish composer Zygmunt Mycielski; the Swiss soprano Flore Wend, now almost permanently an artist in residence in Baltimore at the Peabody Conservatory, but back in Paris for a spell; the devoted Annette Dieudonné and Marcelle de Manziarly, both lifelong friends of Nadia; the indefatigable Winifred Hope Johnstone, now retired and living in France; a former student from Latin America clutching a vast manuscript, to swell the number already covering the dining-room table; and a shy young Japanese girl brought to meet the legendary figure in grey.

While arrangements are made among the inner circle for

future engagements and concerts, the visitors wait until the seat next to Nadia is vacated, occupy it when bidden, and stay there as long as they dare, or until it is made apparent that they must give way to someone else. There is no visible regulation of this procedure, and yet it runs without a hitch. As the day draws on, a maid raises the sunblinds out on the balcony, and the apartment is filled with the golden light of a late Parisian afternoon.

6

Nadia Boulanger's Teachers

When considering Nadia Boulanger as a teacher, one automatically looks first at those who taught her, and at the nature of musical life in the France of her youth. There were two distinct influences. The first, for the organ, was Felix Alexandre Guilmant (1837–1911). His family had been organists and organ-builders in and around Boulogne since the mid-eighteenth century. In 1862, however, when the colossal organ at St Sulpice in Paris was being inaugurated, Guilmant played with distinction and made such an impression that when a successor for Alexis Chauvet was being sought for the Trinité in 1871, Guilmant was offered the post. He then made a series of tours of Europe and America giving recitals that were a huge success, and in 1896 he took over from Widor as professor of organ at the Conservatoire. Widor, incidentally, became organist at St Sulpice in 1869 and remained there for an incredible sixty-four years.

Guilmant was not only a virtuoso organist. He embarked on the publication of his own compositions, acting as his own publisher, and also on two extensive collections of organ music. The first was *L'école classique de l'orgue*, consisting of twenty-five parts published in Paris between 1898 and 1903, and containing works by several foreign composers; and the second was *Archives des maîtres de l'orgue*, ten volumes of music by French composers of the sixteenth, seventeenth and eighteenth centuries, published in Paris and Mainz between 1898 and 1914. This interest in France's own musical history, as well as that of other countries, can only have been beneficial for Guilmant's pupil Nadia Boulanger, especially at a time when pre-

The Villa Medici in Rome — photographed here at the turn of the century — has been the Italian seat of the Académie de France since 1801. Since 1803 winners of the academy's Premier Grand Prix de Rome have received a gold medal and been entitled to take up residence in the Villa Medici for four years.

Nadia Boulanger in 1908, the year she won the Prix de Rome, with some of her fellow competitors. Nadia Boulanger's very participation in what had hitherto been almost exclusively a male event was in itself of great significance let alone the fact that she also won a prize.

Lili Boulanger was the first woman ever to win the Premier Grand Prix de Rome, which she did in 1913.

The fact is often overlooked that in the same year she won another, less glamorous prize, the Prix Lepaulle, with her vocal quartet Renouveau, and was obviously making her presence felt in French music.

Already, however, it was evident to her sister Nadia that she was in need of much devotion, and this Nadia gave unceasingly for the rest of Lili's brief life.

The American Conservatory at Fontainebleau was founded in 1921, in a wing of the palace forming one side of the Cour des Adieux where Napoleon took his farewell after signing his abdication in 1814. Nadia Boulanger taught there from its inception, and in 1950 became director. More than fifty years later, she is still active in its organization.

Nadia Boulanger at the console of the organ in her Paris apartment, a photograph taken in the twenties. It was in 1925 that she gave the first performance of Aaron Copland's Symphony *for organ and orchestra, with Walter Damrosch conducting, and indeed it was as a solo organist, that she first became known to the musical public at large.*

Hand in hand with Nadia Boulanger's devotion to her life of teaching has gone an unswerving devotion to the memory of her beloved sister Lili, and the propagation of her music. This marble bust still stands on the mantel-piece, holding pride of place in the Paris apartment.

Nadia Boulanger's friendship with Igor Stravinsky was probably the most important, in musical terms, in her life, and dated before World War II, in Paris. Naturally she has sustained many musical friendships over the years, of varying degrees of intensity, but Stravinsky's influence on her was of fundamental importance. His respect for her acute musical ear and ability as a conductor was manifestly confirmed when he entrusted to her the first performance of his Dumbarton Oaks *concerto in Washington in 1938.*

On Sunday, September 16th 1962 the first edition of the BBC – tv Monitor *series paid tribute to Nadia Boulanger. Viewers saw her holding a master class, conduct the Ambrosian Singers, talk about music and discuss piano technique. She also compared styles of playing with examples of music by Chopin and Bartók.*
BBC Copyright Photograph.

Romantic music was not in vogue or even very widely known.

Guilmant's first lessons had come from his father, who was born in 1794, and survived until 1890. Nadia's own father, one recalls, was born in 1815, and lived until 1900, and was a friend of Gounod and Ambroise Thomas. One can make too much of such historical successions, but as musical heritages are handed on, they tend to be kept alive. Widor, mentioned earlier, was a pupil in Brussels of Lemmens (1823–1881), himself a pupil of Adolf Friedrich Hesse (1809–1863), a pupil of Forkel (1749–1818), who had worked with C. P. E. Bach (1714–1788), son of the great J. S. Bach. Guilmant also went to Lemmens in Brussels, but only for a month. Forkel has been looked on by some as the father of modern musicology, though this claim is disputed in other quarters.

In 1894 Guilmant was also one of the founders, with Vincent d'Indy and Charles Bordes (1863–1909), of the Schola Cantorum. It began as an association for religious music, and in the following year brought out a magazine, *La Tribune de St Gervais*, of which Bordes was the editor and St Gervais the name of the Paris church of which he was organist. The Schola finally became a teaching institution in 1896, hence the two dates sometimes given for its foundation.

Vincent d'Indy, who was born in 1851, came from an aristocratic and military milieu where music was nevertheless an accepted part of social life. He was destined for a career in law, but soon evinced the talent for music that made him one of the most important musicians of his day. Although the direction of the Schola Cantorum was originally a triumvirate of D'Indy, Guilmant, and Bordes (who specialized in Gregorian chant), D'Indy soon emerged as the real director. The Schola had the specific aim of encouraging the study of church music, but it grew and developed in such a way that it broadened its syllabus and opened new schools – for example, the ones under Bordes at Montpellier and Avignon – and soon became a conservatory of international standing.

Over and above its series of chamber music concerts, it gave hundreds of choral and symphony concerts in a period of three decades, in which then contemporary works by Dukas, Roussel and Debussy were performed, as well as those of much older composers. From the point of view of scholarship, however,

D'Indy did little more than contribute to the general climate, which favoured the rehabilitation of forgotten works. Controversy still rages over the instrumentation of Monteverdi operas, for example: there are basically two schools of thought on the matter, indicating that there is probably still more to be done, if only to convince one side that there is more scope for imagination than its adherents would concede.

Another important point in common between D'Indy and Bordes was their championing of French folk music. Despite the very different nature, both geographically and culturally, of the various regions that combine to make modern France, folk traditions today have only survived in any very marked way in Brittany and Alsace-Lorraine. In the last century there were still living traditions in other areas, however, and some of the tunes collected on the eastern side of the Massif Central as it falls towards the Rhône – for example, the Vivarais and, further south, the Cévennes – were incorporated by D'Indy into his music, or used as basic thematic material.

One tends to think of D'Indy as belonging to the school of César Franck, since he was his pupil, friend, assistant and biographer, but D'Indy also supported Debussy, and stood up for his *Pelléas et Mélisande* at a time when few other people did. Moreover, in a famous concert in Rome, he included Debussy's *Nuages* and *Fêtes*, as a result of which the audience began to shout and whistle. Nothing daunted, D'Indy took up his baton once more and made the orchestra repeat both the works, this time to the applause of the audience.

He worked tirelessly for music, for his pupils, and for the ideals in which he believed. To some he was perhaps too rigid, but he knew as well as any the nature of the problems facing musicians. As a working musician he was incensed by criticism that was ill-informed, simply destructive, or purely a matter of personal opinion. In 1899 he was moved to write:

'I consider criticism absolutely useless; indeed, I should even say injurious . . . Criticism as a rule is the opinion some gentleman or another has of a work. How should such an opinion be of any use to art? However interesting it may be to know the views – even erroneous views – of certain men of genius or even merely of great talent, such as Goethe, Schumann, Wagner, Sainte-Beuve or Michelet, if they condescend to criticism, it leaves one quite indifferent to know whether such and such a gentleman likes or dislikes this or that dramatic or musical work.'

As an indication of the tradition of musical criticism obtaining at that time in France, and still in vogue some sixty or seventy years later – i.e. in 1960 and 1970 – here is an extract from the review of a concert that appeared in *La France Musicale* in 1842: 'X gave in the Salle Pleyel a charming soirée, a fête peopled with adorable smiles, delicate and rosy faces, small and well-formed white hands; a splendid fête where simplicity was combined with grace and elegance, and where good taste served as a pedestal to wealth . . .' The name of the performer on this occasion was Chopin.

Despite periodic revolutions, traditions die hard in France, and only ten years ago it was still almost as important for the reviewer to say who designed the frock worn by the *diva* at her recital the night before as it was to let the readers know what she sang, let alone how she sang it. Criticism of the arts in France has unfortunately tended to be a vehicle for the reviewer to display his erudition, or vent his wrath, rather than a means of enlightening the public about the work in question. One of the amazing things about the early criticisms that Nadia Boulanger wrote for *Le Monde Musical* was the fact that she said how the music was played, and commented on such details as balance and note values, which few other reviewers were mentioning even fifty years later.

Another traditional fundamental to French music, and also one that has been a long time in dying, is that of the salon. On the positive side one must admit at once that generous hostesses, sometimes gifted musicians themselves, have given many young or struggling musicians the opportunity to be heard and to make themselves known. Such families as the Noailles, the Polignacs and the Caraman-Chimays in Belgium have exercised a wide and enlightened patronage, and certainly Nadia Boulanger was one of its beneficiaries. On the debit side, the effect on the music itself has sometimes been stultifying, and the occasions themselves something of an endurance test. Here is Henry James writing to his father in 1876:

'(Madame Viardot-Garcia) has invited me to her musical parties (Thursdays) and to her Sundays *en famille*. I have been to a couple of the former and (as yet only) one of the latter. She herself is a most fascinating and interesting woman, ugly, yet also very handsome or, in the French sense, *très-belle*. Her musical parties are rigidly musical and to me, therefore rigidly boresome, especially as she herself sings very little. I stood the other night on my legs for three hours (from 11 till 2) in a suffocating room, listening to an interminable fiddling, with the only consolation that Gustave Doré, standing beside me, seemed as bored as myself. But when Madame Viardot does sing, it is superb. She sang last time a scene from Gluck's *Alcestis*, which was the finest piece of musical declamation, of a grandly tragic sort, that I can conceive.'

Pauline Viardot was sister to the great dramatic soprano Malibran, and herself a distinguished mezzo-soprano. She had had a triumph with Gluck's *Orpheus* in 1859 and his *Alcestis* in 1861. She gave up the stage in 1863, but sang in concerts until 1870, and then from 1871 until 1875 she taught at the Conservatoire. She had therefore retired only a few months before James heard her. A friend of Turgenev, she lived until 1910.

The Viardot musical salons, despite the boredom for the non-musical, had nevertheless a certain standard and sense of musical integrity most of the time. At its worst, however, the salon was simply another aspect of the ossifying state of French music, with the bones hung on those two pillars of tradition, the Opéra and the Conservatoire. Debussy had some biting words on the former:

'Everybody knows our national Opera House, at least by repute. I can assure you from painful experience that it has not changed. A stranger would take it for a railway station and, once inside, would mistake it for a Turkish bath.

'They continue to produce curious noises which the people who pay call music, but there is no need to believe them implicitly.

'By special permission and a State subsidy this theatre may produce anything; it matters so little what, that elaborately luxurious *loges à salons* have been installed, so called because they are the most convenient places for not hearing anything of the music: they are the last *salons* where conversation still takes place.'

All too often the situation in the salons themselves was little better. Two aspiring singers in Paris in the mid-1960s, one working with Poulenc's friend Pierre Bernac, and the other with Nadia Boulanger, presented a programme of duets and solo songs to a very influential lady in the world of Parisian salons with a view to an engagement. After listening politely but evidently with some boredom to a group of Purcell duets, the great lady remarked: 'Very nice, my dears, but can you not sing some lovely Mendelssohn, or something like the barcarolle from the *Tales of Hoffmann*?' There is a terrible malaise in French music, of which this little instance is all too often a symptom. It has its humorous side, but this only puts it into the category of tragi-comedy, when one thinks that a great deal of French musical life is still controlled in this way. Some of the words spoken by Lady Bracknell in Oscar Wilde's *The Importance of being Earnest* still ring horribly true: 'one wants something that will encourage conversation, particularly at the end of the season when every one has practically said whatever they had to say, which, in most cases, was probably not much.' To which her nephew Algernon replies: 'Of course the music is a great difficulty. You see, if one plays good music people don't listen, and if one plays bad music people don't talk.'

It was in reaction to this situation that Boulez and his friends founded *Le Domaine Musical* in 1953–4, but it still persisted, to the point where one was reluctantly forced to conclude that the French were a markedly unmusical people. Yet they produced a stream of brilliant composers and performers equal to any in the world at one time. Part of the trouble may be a result of the marked division between folk music and the aristocratic or courtly music that grew up with the increasing strength of the monarchy and lasted until virtually the end of the eighteenth century, the various schools of music adopting it as an academic subject like any other. There is certainly a marked lack in France of that famous gifted amateur so prevalent in, for example, English music, but by no means intended here in any pejorative sense. Also the virtual collapse of the French ecclesiastical musical tradition has left a gap that is unlikely to be filled. The brilliance of the French organ school in the second half of the nineteenth century should not blind us to the agony of its choral tradition at the same time, so that by 1919 Nadia Boulanger could deplore the lack of performances of the great choral repertoire in Parisian concerts. With the benefit of hindsight we can now see that, although much of the apparatus of church music was still intact in the early decades of the present century, its vogue and standards were nevertheless on the decline.

One might even go so far as to say that without the great talent of its organists, church music in France might well have died much sooner. Certainly in England and other countries of continental Europe – one thinks especially of Germany, Holland and Belgium – the church still continues to play a large part in the musical life of the country, as it did in France at the end of the last century. Nadia Boulanger was initially an essential part of the French church music tradition. There has always been an organ in her Paris apartment. She played César Franck's *Prélude* and *Finale* for organ (from his *Six Pièces* of 1860–62) at a concert in Paris as early as 1918, and it is fitting that when she went to America in 1925, she played, at its world première, the Symphony for Organ and Orchestra specially written for her by Aaron Copland. This was given in New York by the Boston Symphony Orchestra under Walter Damrosch on 11 January 1925. Despite her convictions about the merit of the composition, Walter Damrosch declared: 'If a young man, at the age of twenty-three, can write a symphony like that, in five years he will be ready to commit murder.' It was the unpleasant nature of the harmonies that had provoked this remark. Virgil Thomson wrote, however: 'I found this work at that time deeply moving, even to tears, for its way of saying things profoundly for our generation.'

The other person who taught Nadia Boulanger was not especially a composer for organ, or indeed primarily an organist, although he was choirmaster at the Madeleine in Paris from 1877 and then became organist there in 1896. Gabriel Fauré (1845–1924) showed his talent for music at a very early age, and when he was only nine years old was sent by his parents on a scholarship to Paris, to the Ecole Niedermeyer, which had been founded especially for classical and religious music in 1853 – or rather was the refounding of an older school that had closed during the Revolution of 1830. Fauré spent eleven years with Niedermeyer, learning the basis of his intended profession of choirmaster and organist, but a new impetus was given to the young man's musical education when Niedermeyer died in 1861 and Saint-Saëns became Fauré's piano teacher at the school.

For Fauré Saint-Saëns opened up the music of Schumann, Liszt and Wagner, as well as his own, and as a friend watched over Fauré's first attempts at composition. In fact he remained attached to Fauré for the rest of his life. Before he was twenty-one Fauré left the school and was engaged as organist of the church of St Saveur in Rennes, beginning in January 1866. Thus began a pattern, which was to persist for twenty-five years, of earning a meagre living as a church musician, supplementing his income with private lessons, and following his real bent as a composer almost as a subsidiary occupation.

In 1870 he returned to Paris, where he held a succession of posts as organist, until in 1877 he was appointed choirmaster at the Madeleine in succession to Dubois, professor of harmony at the Conservatoire, who had just been appointed organist. Fauré was to follow in Dubois' footsteps for the rest of his career, even replacing him eventually as Director of the Conservatoire. Fauré also returned to the Ecole Niedermeyer in that year as a permanent member of the staff.

At this stage Fauré still had not composed a great deal of music, apart from some songs, but already his skill as a pianist – both as an accompanist and improviser – allied to his charm and urbanity, gained him a considerable following in the salons of Parisian society. In 1872 Saint-Saëns had introduced him to the Viardot family, where he quickly became one of the inner circle. He fell in love with one of Pauline Viardot's daughters, Marianne, and for four years he courted her, until they were engaged in 1877. Unfortunately the engagement was of short duration, and Fauré was deeply hurt.

Saint-Saëns once more came to the rescue, inviting Fauré to accompany him at the end of the year to Weimar, where Liszt was putting on *Samson et Dalila*. The next year Fauré went to Cologne to hear *Das Rheingold* and *Die Walküre*, and in 1879 to Munich, where he attended rehearsals of the whole of *The Ring*. So much exposure to Wagner left little or no traces in Fauré's music, but it may well have released his creative energies, for 1879 was the beginning of a period which, over the space of twenty years, established Fauré as a composer of the first rank.

The death of his father in 1886 and that of his mother in 1888 inspired his *Requiem* (1887–8), which marked a renewal of French religious music. A visit to Venice in 1891 represented a break in the monotony of Fauré's existence, and inspired the five songs to poems by Verlaine. Relief was on the way, however, for in 1892 Fauré was appointed Inspector of the French provincial conservatories, which led to a good deal of travel and freed him from the exhausting task of giving lessons to supplement his income. One of his most successful works, the suite of songs to poems of Verlaine entitled *La bonne chanson*, dates from this period (1892–3).

When Dubois became Director of the Conservatoire in 1896, Fauré became organist at the Madeleine, and professor of composition at the Conservatoire in succession to Massenet. Nadia Boulanger was, for a time, assistant organist at the Madeleine.

In the nine years he held his teaching post at the Conservatoire – until 1905 – Fauré tried in his instructions to be as undogmatic as possible. As Charles Koechlin put it, 'the most effective aspect of his teaching depended on an emulation that he incited of his own accord, through the supreme quality of his art'. One might say this about his music, too. It never browbeats or bludgeons the listener into submission; it speaks, and in so doing either makes its point or leaves the listener cold.

In 1905 Fauré succeeded Dubois as Director of the Conservatoire, a post he retained until 1920. As professor of composition he had inherited from his predecessor, Massenet, pupils such as Florent Schmitt, Aubert, Enesco and Koechlin, and he added to them Nadia Boulanger, Roger-Ducasse, Ladmirault, Vuillermoz, Casella and, probably the most famous of all, Ravel. It was to Fauré, '*mon cher maître*', that Ravel dedicated his string quartet. The appointment was something of a departure, since Fauré had never been a pupil of the Conservatoire, and had not won the Prix de Rome. He at last opened the doors of the establishment to currents that had been active in French music for the previous thirty years or more.

In his lifetime Fauré more or less presided over the division of French music into two distinct streams. One led from Chabrier and Debussy through his pupils Schmitt and Ravel to the Six (Honegger, Poulenc, Milhaud, Durey, Auric and Tailleferre), Jolivet, and – at the present time – to Messiaen, who now presides over the organ at the Trinité. The other stream went from Franck and Chausson to Vincent d'Indy, Dukas, and Roussel. From both these streams Fauré stands somewhat apart musically, but he remains nonetheless a quintessentially French composer.

In 1871 he was a founder member, with Saint-Saëns, Franck, Lalo and others, of the Société Nationale de Musique, whose aim was to propagate contemporary French music. In a re-markably short space of time they were able to get works by young composers included in the programmes of the large public concerts, which hitherto had been closed to them. In 1898, for example, they organised a concert of Ravel's works, and it was at one of their concerts at the Schola Cantorum on 5 March 1904 that the first performance of his quartet in F was given. It is interesting that five years previously, in 1899, Ravel had used whole-tone scales in his music, which helps to put the advent of dodecaphony into perspective. It was not the aim of the society to be deliberately avant-garde, however.

The danger of such an organization as the Société Nationale de Musique, of course, was that in promoting French music alone, much that would be of value to French musicians from abroad might be overlooked. Fauré was sufficiently aware of this to become president of another society in 1909, the Société Musicale Indépendante, whose committee included Stravinsky and Bartók. The society aimed to be cosmopolitan in its ap-proach, though not to the extent of excluding French works, and Milhaud's string quartets were first heard there. At the same time, the Société Nationale blossomed out into Strauss and Russian music, and the two societies continued to co-exist.

It was a great tragedy for Fauré that when he reached the summit of his career – following on the Ravel scandal over the Prix de Rome, as we saw earlier, in 1905 – he was already aware that he was having difficulty in hearing; this alone would have been a great disadvantage, but he also began to experience dis-tortion in the sound that he could hear. Some have tended to see this trouble as the direct cause of the change that came over his music in his last works, since they have lost all the suavity of his earlier music; but bearing in mind the late Beethoven quartets, also written under this sort of handicap, one may regard Fauré's later work as a distillation of his writing. In any case, even if a trained musician cannot hear notes as played or sung – and colds or similar infections often impair the hearing – he knows in his inner ear what the notes should sound like, and ought to be able to go on composing.

One imagines Fauré as a benign and infinitely courteous man, mellowed by the experience of years of teaching, and finally receiving recognition for the monotonous and demanding earlier part of his life when the rewards were meagre. It never apparently made him bitter, or sour, and his pupils were for the most part devoted to him. He was essentially practical in musical matters, however, and capable of forthright replies. When Gide asked him, somewhat pretentiously, one suspects, what tempo his song *Clair de lune* ought to be taken at, Fauré replied: 'It all depends on the voice. When I don't like the voice I speed up the tempo.' One has a sudden glimpse of the interminable auditions to which Fauré must have been subjected throughout his life, and the agonies he must have had to bear in the process.

Gabriel Fauré was one of the most important influences on Nadia Boulanger. She regarded it a privilege to be a pupil of his. He was a close friend of the family, and yet she recalls that she never heard him talk about his music, or about the problems he had latterly with his hearing. In this respect Nadia is very similar. Inquiries about her health, though never ignored in any way that might be regarded as rude, are nonetheless quickly disposed of, and inquiries then made about the visitor or a mutual friend.

There was obviously much in Fauré's approach to the teaching of music that struck a chord in Nadia Boulanger's mind. While trying to be as undogmatic as possible, and in this she is at one with Fauré, Nadia Boulanger believes that every student must be as well equipped as possible to carry out the profession he has chosen. Her role as teacher is therefore to provide the pupil with the means of equipping himself, and guiding and advising – possibly brusquely at times. In the last resort this is the only way in which the student's own musical personality will form and emerge as truly his.

Historically Nadia Boulanger came at a very opportune moment. French music had reacted against Romanticism, and was therefore placed in a very advantageous position to welcome the new developments of the twentieth century. The school of Franck is an exception, but basically French music during the Romantic period was always looking towards ideals that one would term classical by comparison with, say, the French art of the period. In her own mind she always sought after a distillation of expression that was more in sympathy with classicism than romanticism. She was on the side of those who looked outwards, rather than in.

This was the musical background from which Nadia Boulanger came. Since she first began to teach, Paris has lost what few claims it still had to being one of the musical capitals of the world. Indeed as a musical nation the French seem to have been crossing a vast desert for some time. They still produce performers of great eminence, though few great singers, but the really creative minds in music have usually had to leave France before they have fully realized their potential and won the acclaim they deserve. It is much to Nadia Boulanger's credit that she began to spread her teaching further afield long before this happened, and recognized where her talents would be best employed.

7

The Basis of Nadia Boulanger's Teaching

Although Nadia Boulanger does not have any particular method, or way of teaching that she has perfected for herself, and which is peculiar to her, she nevertheless stresses some fundamental elements without which, in her estimation, one cannot even begin to think of a musical career. When a pupil comes to her, especially a would-be composer, she usually wants to know first what his musical ear is like. She decided that Lennox Berkeley's was good, that he had a natural ear in fact. This was obviously a great advantage, and meant that he could concentrate on the aspects that were less strong, such as fugue and counterpoint. With other pupils, however, Nadia Boulanger regrets that they come to study harmony before they can really hear, and dissociate, the different notes of the chord. They can hear the chord as a whole, of course, but do not know exactly what it represents in terms of individual notes. One way for a teacher to try and help a student with the problem is to encourage improvisation at the keyboard, or learning keyboard harmony, so as to build up his sense of harmonic structure.

Nadia Boulanger, however, tends to make her students do what they are probably quite justified in regarding as boring, traditional exercises, such as building up cadences by playing first the bass note, then the tenor, then the alto and finally the soprano, and with no more than four chords. Then they can perhaps play one or two parts on the piano, and sing a third, and so isolate what seem to be the vertical elements in the chord but which are in fact horizontal, as the harmonic texture moves along.

It was her very practical approach to the business of learning the musician's trade – or, from her point of view, teaching it – that enabled her to accept as a pupil the American jazz musician Quincy Jones.

Jones was born in Chicago in 1933, and took up the trumpet at the age of fourteen. He began to take lessons, and in 1951 won a music scholarship. He played in Lionel Hampton's band for about two years, and late in 1953 he turned freelance in New York. By this time he was writing music and making band arrangements for recording sessions, for Ray Anthony's band in particular. At the age of twenty-one he was regarded as one of the greatest arrangers in his field, but he was not satisfied and decided to go to Paris to study with Nadia Boulanger. Not surprisingly, some of the things he has said and written – such as 'Music is the one language you don't have to translate' – closely echo some of Nadia Boulanger's beliefs.

His experience as a trumpet player has stood him in good stead as an arranger. As he himself said: 'I like to look at the orchestra as my personal instrument, the same as the soloist looks at his, and I like to improvise with it. I like to describe my feelings, my moods and my thoughts, so that writing becomes the same as improvising a solo for me.'

This is very close to the Boulanger idea of making composing a habit, so that the composer evolves the practice of expressing his musical thoughts as easily as he might write a letter. One also finds in Quincy Jones's writing the Boulanger concern for the balance between the head and the heart in music:

'I like to have the feeling of an improvisation in the writing. The only way to write this feeling into a score is to let the head and the heart work together. If the head works alone the score usually sounds contrived, even with the best craftsmanship. If the heart works with the head, though, the score becomes more of a living thing. All your feelings are able to flow freely. All your thoughts too. In effect, you tell the truth about yourself, and the truth doesn't need to hurt. Jazz has always been a man telling the truth about himself.'

What is essential to any musician, but to composers most of all, is the ability to hear music accurately. As Nadia Boulanger has said: 'Many people, gifted musicians, do not hear. Their ear is not trained and you have to persuade them, which is difficult – in some cases it's hard, they suffer. They fail to understand that their freedom depends entirely on establishing the spontaneity between what they hear in their inner ear and what they can write down.'

For her, *solfeggio* dominates the whole system, and the word *solfeggio* means writing, hearing and seeing accurately whatever notes come into the composer's head. For this she regards Hindemith's *Elementary Training for Musicians* as an essential book. In her own words: 'Nobody will ever persuade me one can be ignorant of it.' The book begins in a deceptively easy and basic way, and yet within its 237 pages contains much that many practising musicians would like to have mastered.

Certainly the French have incredible ability at knowing their *solfeggio*, and their ability at sight reading, particularly that of the singers, is the particular envy of their English counterparts. Tonic solfa has never been a very satisfactory method of teaching sight reading in England, because the starting note of each key is taken as Doh, and therefore any note of the scale can be Doh. *Solfeggio* in France keeps Doh on C, and this gives a fixed point to which all keys may be related.

Nadia Boulanger believes that a pupil must have a properly trained ear so that he can have total freedom to write or play. Doubtless because she has such a good ear herself, and such an analytic mind when reading a score, she would like all her students to be able to dissect chords, and be fully aware of what they hear. For one thing, she feels that harmony may only be an adjunct to the fundamental structure: 'Nice little lace – take off lace, and life will go on the same.' She feels that accretion of harmony may hide unworthiness of line itself in music.

As an example she cites the slow movement of Beethoven's piano trio in B flat – the 'Archduke'. Here she finds the writing so perfect that to change one note in one of the chords would be to spoil everything. Of course, when writing for such limited forces, each single note tells far more in the general effect than a note in a work for full orchestra. Even so, one cannot deny the harmonic element, and Nadia Boulanger is the first to admit that in overemphasizing the melodic line at the expense of the secondary, but nevertheless essential, harmonic element, one would risk betraying the music and with it the composer's intentions. Although one can, for study purposes, play Stravinsky or the Beethoven quartets at the piano, the disposition of the notes in the various instrumental parts is so vital that the whole effect is ruined. As an example, she quotes the closing chord of Stravinsky's Symphony of Psalms, where the whole effect, for her, turns on the disposition of the one note in the oboe, without which the whole would not exist.

Such an approach creates several problems, particularly in the teacher-pupil relationship. When presented with a piece of music that a pupil has written, the teacher must first ascertain that what is on the paper is what the pupil intended to write. The teacher may point out what he or she considers to be mistakes, or certainly not particularly happy moments in the writing, and the pupil may think again. On the other hand, he may well make a stand and say that the music was exactly what he intended; and if it is a piece of free composition and not a traditional exercise, then in the last resort the teacher can only give an opinion as to what, in his or her consideration, would have been better, and there the matter must rest.

Lennox Berkeley recalls that she was always writing on his exercises – as she did with those of Marcelle de Manziarly – under places that she had underlined, or where she had put a cross because there was a mistake. Very often, he recalls, she wrote: 'Very musical, but forbidden'. He could not help thinking at the time that it was sad that it should be forbidden if it was so musical. However, he managed to be philosophical about it, because he felt, and still feels, that there is no point in undertaking a discipline unless you are prepared to abide by the rules.

Not all students were able to accept this, and when one of them had the temerity to point out that what J. S. Bach did all the time in his music was what the student was being criticized for, she retorted: 'He can, but you cannot.' Evidently it takes a certain kind of temperament to accept this working method, and if one of Nadia Boulanger's pupils has not that temperament, it is unlikely that he will feel he is getting very far.

She admits that she is a hard taskmaster: 'I demand all that I can. I always try to demand more. I feel I never demand enough. You must respect people enough to expect from them a great constant effort to develop all that brings them the freedom of expression. We come back to the beginning again, and we come to the conclusion with it – give them the means of expressing themselves.' Only in this way will the composer be confident that what he writes down is what he intended to say.

Naturally, when it comes to the performance of a work, a composer may well be forced to admit that what he heard in his inner ear may not work in practice, or be extremely difficult to bring off successfully every time. He may therefore prefer to modify what he has written, and this may be something even a very experienced composer is obliged to do in varying acoustic conditions, or given the differing qualities of voices or instruments.

In the present climate of increasing noise pollution, however, one may well wonder whether this is not a somewhat academic approach. Pop music is played so loudly that one wonders whether younger generations will ever be able to hear subtle musical effects at all, and melody and rhythm have been debased to such a point that, by comparison, the Beatles seem like masters of classical music. Added to this is the tendency of some contemporary classical composers to be very lax about the notes they write, to the point where it seems almost a matter of choice for the performers. Obviously if the written music presents severe technical problems, a composer may well be able to modify what he has written so as to accommodate his performers, but it cannot say much for his ear if he more or less allows performers to rewrite the music themselves. Even less credible is the fashion for aleatoric music, where a composer simply indicates passages for the performers to improvise on – say a given set of notes. This is all very well if the performers are capable of improvising to some effect that has artistic value, and is stylistically suitable to the music itself; but all too often they are not really prepared for such a venture, as musically democratic as it may be, and the value of such an exercise, and its effect on the listener, are questionable.

One can draw parallels with ornamentation, which was left entirely to the performer, but then it was always done within fairly strictly defined limits, and there were conventions everyone knew and understood. Even at their most florid they were essentially intended as a complement to the music, even as an extension of it, but improvisation in the actual material on the part of the performer was unthinkable.

Interpolation was a different matter, and one which, since the Romantic movement, we no longer indulge in. Now we treat each work, whether it be an opera or symphony, as an artistic entity, and would not dream of adding arias from other operas or movements from other symphonies simply because we liked them. This has also been reflected in the change that has taken place even in the last fifty years in concert programmes. Today a symphony concert will probably consist of three main works, or possibly four, but they will all be given in their entirety. Fifty years ago, however, it was fairly common to find odd arias or movements of works being given in the course of a concert, and Mozart rubbing shoulders with Rimsky-Korsakov. There are some who are always liable to overcompensate, of course, and approach the classical repertoire with too much reverence. In fact one of the less admirable legacies of Romanticism has been to put the composer on an artistic pinnacle, which may well turn out to be an ivory tower. Nowadays this is rarely of the composer's own choosing, since it would seem to exist more in the minds of the concertgoing public than the composers themselves.

The Wagner image of the composer as a being living on a higher plane than most other mortals, and therefore not subject to exactly the same restraint, has now disappeared. Most composers would now maintain that they want their music to appeal to people, and often that means the populace at large. Sometimes they even see their music as having a political message to convey or a role to play in society. Even so, in the last analysis it is the musician who speaks, and that will be essentially a personal voice.

Between the composer and the listener, however, come the interpreters of the music – performers and the conductor. It is their responsibility to speak for the composer, and it is in their power to do it faithfully or unfaithfully. Nadia Boulanger has concerned herself with performers as well as composers, and has worked with some particularly distinguished interpreters.

In the course of a musician's career he may be called on to interpret anything from a vast repertoire. He may try to assimilate the elements of the majority of styles he is likely to encounter, or he may decide to specialize in one particular field – which is all very well if by his choice he can get enough work to provide himself with a living. But today, with more and more musicians chasing less and less work, the pressure to accept almost any offer of work is enormous. Naturally the truly great artists are at liberty to choose, as long as they are at the top of their form, but rank and file musicians are not so lucky.

When it comes to performance, a conductor worth his salt will tell his performers at the outset how he is going to interpret the music under rehearsal, and make known his preference for ornamentation if and when appropriate. Even so, the performer, if only for his own satisfaction, is more likely to interpret a work better if he understands it, and this is especially true for soloists.

The violinist Henryk Szeryng studied with Nadia Boulanger, and recalls the way in which she tried to explain to instrumentalists the importance of analysing works and knowing exactly what the meaning of each musical subject was, and the different ramifications of the harmony. In particular, he remembered studying Szymanowski's violin concerto Op 61, written in 1932–3, a few years before the composer's death. Nadia Boulanger asked him to make an analysis of the work, which took him several weeks to complete, for he not only looked at the music from the point of view of rhythm, harmony and melody, but he knew instinctively that she also expected him to consider the thematic content, in particular the folk element, and indeed the very sources of the composition. Almost any instrumentalist will analyse a piece of music harmonically when he is memorizing it, and in this way he can use modulations from one key to another as signposts when it comes to performance, assuming that it is a work in traditional tonality, of course. To go deeper, however, is obviously going to enhance and amplify his appreciation of the music and the composer's intentions, and therefore make him ultimately a more faithful interpreter of them.

For singers the problem is perhaps less acute, or rather less tends to be expected of them when it comes to analysis of the work. There is no reason, however, why this should deter them from trying to understand the music as much as possible. There is still a feeling in the musical world that singers are somewhat inferior to instrumentalists, since very often they have a beautiful voice and little more. But one can see that musical intelligence allied to a beautiful voice is much to be desired, and indeed a singer who is musically intelligent can often make up for a less than beautiful voice. It is a pleasure to listen to a glorious voice, but if it is no more than that, the pleasure may pall. If we are aware, on the other hand, that a singer has thought carefully about what he is singing, and unfolds an intellectual experience for us as well, then our attention is likely to be held for much longer. We feel that we are being asked to participate, not simply to sit back and indulge ourselves in an aural sensation.

Vocal music has always been very important to Nadia Boulanger. As she has said of it: 'Nothing can replace the voice. The voice is the most important and marvellous thing. I don't know if you have attended a rehearsal of Menuhin. He will sing suddenly what he wants of the orchestra. He sings only a few notes; the whole orchestra has understood.'

She has always had a great admiration for the English contralto Kathleen Ferrier, and frequently uses her recordings to illustrate her analysis classes on Wednesday afternoons. Of Ferrier's recording of Brahms' *Sapphische Ode* she has said: 'I cannot hear this record without tears in the eyes. It is something so unforgettable and wonderful.'

Nadia Boulanger has always made her pupils sing whenever possible, and ensemble singing has been an integral part of their studies. Her formation of a group to perform the Monteverdi recording of 1937 showed early on her ability to weld singers into a body, even when their talents might be of very varying kinds. While she was in America, she organized a concert in May 1942 for the Co-ordinating Council of French Relief Societies. The programme covered an immense range of French concerted vocal music, from early anonymous composers through Jannequin and Rameau to Berlioz, Debussy and Ravel, with some Poulenc thrown in for good measure. The singers had given their services for the evening, but to achieve a balance had to sing softly most of the time, which is very demanding and very tiring for any prolonged period. Virgil Thomson, reviewing the concert, wrote:

'To have produced a balance out of so unmatched an ensemble is a triumph of musicianship on Miss Boulanger's part. To have achieved in addition musical renderings of the highest intelligibility for some of the most difficult music in the world is proof that the great French pedagogue is not fooling around in the dark with regard to musical scores. Like Toscanini, she knows what notes mean in terms of sound. Music is her language and she speaks it.'

Of course Virgil Thomson had little or no need to be persuaded of his former teacher's abilities, but he rightly pointed out that her performances were professional without being theatrical. She established a relationship with her audiences that was friendly and informal, and yet serious. As he continued: 'We are not used to musicianship that is at the same time so gentle and so firm, especially in this age when musicians do everything in the world with music except to speak it as a language and everything to an audience except to say to it in musical language simple and serious things.'

She also communicated the joy that she herself felt in the music. Bernard Keeffe said of the Monteverdi recordings:

'Their impact was, I think, in the vivid enjoyment of the music that was conveyed. I think that most people expected this old music to be academic and dull, and in fact, to be honest, most of us knew it only by examples, usually wrongly printed, in histories of music. Nadia Boulanger revealed a master as vital in his way as her beloved Stravinsky.'

Though one must work hard, and struggle with things that are difficult, one must try to enjoy the act of interpretation even if one cannot enjoy the music itself. Moreover, one is more likely to be able to do this if one has a sound technical basis from which to start. A Bach *da capo* aria may be almost as difficult in its central section as a piece of unaccompanied dodecaphonic music; the harmony seems to disintegrate, and were one to analyse some of the chords, it would seem improbable that they could have been written in the seventeenth or eighteenth centuries. If the singer looks at the direction that the harmonic development is taking, however, the bewildering proliferation of notes then takes on some purpose, and one works through the material with the composer and emerges in the home key once more. This still does not prevent some Bach arias from going on apparently *ad nauseam*, as Anna Russell would say, but it at least makes the likelihood of something being conveyed to the audience more probable.

The Basis of Nadia Boulanger's Teaching

As one of Nadia Boulanger's more recent students has said, when a fellow student was struggling with a multi-voiced canon and experiencing considerable difficulty, she yelled 'Smile'. Later, when the student had the independent voices under control, she very charmingly asked him, as he played on: 'And did you walk through the forest today and appreciate the beauty of nature?' In the last resort the music, for her, must remain on the human plane; otherwise it has failed.

Perhaps her most fruitful relations with performers have been with pianists, and the keyboard is the domain in which she may legitimately claim to know what she is talking about. She was first known, after all, as a recital organist, and when she was teaching at the Conservatoire, she ran a course modestly entitled piano accompaniment, as well as harmony classes. But this course in reality meant improvising from a figured bass in any style, and the ability to read orchestral scores – even the most modern – at the keyboard, making a piano arrangement instantly as she was playing it. She made her pupils play from old editions of Bach, with all the various clefs imaginable, and they had to be able to play without having to stop and think. Nowadays musicians tend to use only the treble and bass clefs, though viola and 'cello players, for example, may use other clefs quite often.

The purpose of the clef is to keep as much of the music as possible on the stave. This makes the music more compact, and prevents the performer from having to work out what the notes would be if they were on leger lines, i.e. additional lines above or below the stave. By the addition of a clef – alto or tenor, for example – the composer can use the stave as a kind of sliding grid, where it will encompass the greatest number of notes in the melody, and keep the most notes on the five lines of the stave.

Apart from the facility it might offer, there is no particular virtue in being able to manipulate clefs, unless one is going to specialize in music where they occur often. Once acquired, however, it is a facility one tends not to lose. Nadia Boulanger never lost hers, and this, combined with her incredible ear, gave her a truly remarkable ability to look at almost any piece of music and be able to read it and play it at once. She has never been interested in virtuosity simply for its own sake, however. It is simply a means to an end, namely the interpretation of the music.

In a way it is akin to the training of an athlete. Almost any exercise that will keep the muscles toned up and the limbs supple has a utility in the function of keeping the whole body in a state of readiness for the tasks it might be called upon to perform. Once this basic fitness has been achieved, any particular skill the athlete wants to acquire is that much nearer his grasp. But the exercises never become an end in themselves.

As one might expect from someone who is such a skilled score reader at the keyboard, Nadia Boulanger is a pianist of considerable stature. She has always been surrounded by pianists, whether of the international calibre of Clifford Curzon or the extremely gifted amateur Princess Irene of Greece. Mention has already been made of the Turkish pianist Idil Biret, but perhaps one of the most fruitful collaborations that Nadia Boulanger ever experienced was with the Romanian Dinu Lipatti. In fact Ernest Ansermet described Nadia Boulanger as Dinu Lipatti's spiritual mother, and his early death was a sad blow to her. In 1937, when he was only twenty, they made a recording of Brahms waltzes Op 39, which reveals not only their remarkable feeling for rhythm, but also their close understanding when performing together. As Nadia Boulanger has said:

'When Lipatti entered on the stage something happened. He played and the whole atmosphere – you cannot describe what it represented. Something – again, no more Lipatti, no more Bach himself, only the music and only the spirit of the music, to a degree indescribable. But behind that . . . that is the great mystery of the world, it is the great mystery of genius given to one man and to very few men. And the possibility to feel this genius for many people – but we cannot talk of that, I am not qualified to talk of that.'

What she has always been qualified to talk on, however, has been – among other things – performances of the piano repertoire, which she has always done with understanding. Her criticism has almost always been constructive. Reviewing a concert in January 1920, for example, she wrote:

'Mlle Dehelly played the Schumann Concerto [at one of the Concerts Colonne] with great relaxation. Some of the entries at the upper end of the keyboard were occasionally somewhat hard, but the overall interpretation bore witness to remarkable virtuosity. The concern to sacrifice the first beats to the benefit of the musical phrase has remained with me, and my belief is that when considered again from this point of view, the interpretation would gain in freedom and depth.'

Rhythm has always been one of Nadia Boulanger's great concerns. We find her returning to it time and time again. As a basic musical knowledge is fundamental to the liberation of a person's musical character, so a basic rhythmic sense is fundamental to a free interpretation of a work, because one can only vary a rhythm when one has a firmly established rhythm in one's head – otherwise there is no rhythm at all.

Writing in December 1946, this time reviewing a performance of Franck's Symphonic Variations, Nadia Boulanger pointed out that what was difficult in a work of this nature was to establish a continuity, and only give details a place in accordance with their importance in the ensemble. While recognizing the pianist's qualities, Nadia Boulanger now advised her to look for the *grande ligne*. She would then understand that once technique has been mastered, all her attention should be focused on the structure of the work and – a feature on which she said she was unable to insist enough – the regularity and certainty of the tempo.

She would frequently cite Stravinsky's feeling for tempo as an example of what she aimed at. It was rigorous and strict, and yet it was absolutely free. In particular she would mention his conducting of the slow movement of his Symphony in Four Movements, or his playing of his *Capriccio*, where his *rubato* defied imitation. *Rubato* means literally 'robbed', and in music a slight variation in the strict value of the notes as an aid to expressiveness. To give a slight feeling of urgency one might move on faster, and to emphasize a particular tonal effect one might hold the music back slightly. Within a much shorter space of time – within one musical phrase – *rubato* does just this, so that in addition to loudness and softness, rich harmonies or open texture, the expressive nature of the music is heightened.

All too often, however, *rubato* tends to lead to sloppy rhythm. As one teacher said: 'If you rob here, then you must pay back again later.' In other words, although there is freedom within the phrase itself, the basic pulse must remain constant. Or as Boulanger herself has said: 'Loose is not beautiful – loose is loose.' Our tendency, she maintains, is to forget that rhythm is something that is forever leading us on. We may well count, and take the metronome, but unless we listen carefully, we find that we fall behind, and lose time. The metronome seems to be wrong, because, unless we pay attention, we lose that fraction of a second that makes such a difference to the whole work. If you have a feeling for constant rhythm, you are carried forward, and you then experience the amazing revelation of the difference between time and rhythm. Time simply goes on, but rhythm has a dynamic impulse.

Again it is to Stravinsky that she automatically turns by way of illustration, but also sometimes to De Falla, whose demonstration of a particular rhythm in the Seven Songs she made him repeat over and over again, because for her it was a revelation, the movement of the planets, life itself. She was amazed to discover, shortly after his death, that his second suite of music from the *Three-cornered Hat* had just been heard in Paris at a concert for the first time. It therefore became a kind of tribute to him, and in his music, in addition to its rhythm and finesse, she praised his dignity – a dignity she also found in his life. 'Listen once again,' she said, 'to the Seven Spanish Songs, or the slow movement of the Harpsichord Concerto, and you will understand exactly which flame has been extinguished, exactly *who* has gone away from us.'

Nadia Boulanger could be generous in appreciation even when she did not particularly like the music – Yvonne Loriod playing Schönberg, for instance – because she could always see beyond the immediate circumstances to the talents and application that the performance of a potentially unrewarding piece of music – unrewarding to her – might easily conceal. And of course if there was a combination of a brilliant pianist and a work of which she approved, as with George Chavchavadze playing Beethoven's Fourth Piano Concerto, then her admiration knew no bounds.

Despite her praise for the vocalists or instrumentalists, Nadia Boulanger has never underestimated the essential part played by the conductor in the performance of music. In some respects his is the hardest task of all, because he is responsible for the interpretation; yet only if the players or singers are responding to him, can he make any impression at all. He can rehearse, advise, admonish, know the score backwards, but all this is of no avail whatsoever when it comes to the actual performance. He depends on the composer on the one hand to write the music and the performers on the other to sing or play it. He must therefore take control of the situation, impress himself upon the performers, and bring to the music all his skill, technique and acquired knowledge.

Conducting has also been very important in Nadia Boulanger's life. She was often brought to the attention of many concertgoers for the first time as a conductor, a role which, until her advent, had been an exclusively male prerogative. It is difficult to know whether her conducting sprang from her conception of music, or whether conducting enhanced that conception. The two are certainly very closely allied, because of her all-pervading quest for the *grande ligne*. Any conflict that a conductor might experience between the shaping of the melodic lines and the emphasizing of the harmonic structure is resolved for her in the ensemble, which is achieved when one has understood the work totally. The discovery of the *grande ligne* and its interpretation makes everything else fall into place:

'. . . it is an ensemble – an ensemble which represents ideally such an intelligence, such a knowledge, such a submission to the work, such a mastery of means for communicating this understanding to the orchestra, which represents also the great magnetism which exists in the conductor. He has a way to make, to understand his thoughts, to transmit it to the others.

'I remember one unforgettable performance of the D major Brahms in Bucharest with Barbirolli; when he finished the whole orchestra had played for him, every note. I've seldom seen such a thing. And when I went to see him after the concert he was still moved at what had happened, and I was profoundly moved because it struck me it was a complete fusion between the members of the orchestra and the conductor. A point of view did not exist. It was the deep understanding, the understanding which dominates the knowledge, dominates understanding, dominates the means to obtain that, to arrive, to let the work come to its complete expression, to its complete being.'

She then quoted the occasion when someone asked Toscanini about conducting and his musical life in general, and said what joys he must have experienced in the course of it. He looked at his wife and said that on two or three occasions the orchestra had given him exactly what he wanted, and his wife gave the exact dates, which stretched over a period of forty years. As Nadia Boulanger commented: 'Three dates when the miracle has happened, when everything was there, when the complete forgetfulness of oneself was achieved, when suddenly the music itself is left alone.'

One of the essential elements of conducting, as with all music, is that of rhythm. With characteristic incisiveness she roundly condemns lazy rhythm, but in a more reflective mood:

'It is a question – a terribly difficult question. The difference between being in time or having rhythm, which is quite different; it's an inner pulse and for me the greatest example I have is of having heard so often with Stravinsky, playing new works of his. And he was counting, and the way he counted, I said to him fifty times, "Please make a recording so that people realise what counting means, what is the succession in time, the growing in time, the gaining on time". It was rigorous, it was strict and absolutely free.'

Of course the concept of *rubato*, as we have already seen, is possibly one of the most misunderstood in the whole of music, but when one hears proper *rubato* it gives the music a lift, a dimension one had scarcely envisaged. But, underneath, the basic pulse has to be as steady as a rock.

As well as being concerned with good rhythm, she had always been interested in unusual rhythm. Aaron Copland said:

'I can remember one of the first things Boulanger remarked upon, when I was her student, was the rather curious rhythm that I was using. They were generally groups of three and five eighth notes. It was a kind of slow fox-trot rhythm . . . now that particular little rhythmic grouping I don't think she had seen in quite that way. And then I was doing a little poly-rhythmic thing, with the bass doing a steady rhythm of one kind and the rest of the music doing other rhythms, which also struck her as rather odd. It was the first time that anyone had ever given me the notion that I had any special feeling for rhythm, different from anybody else's.'

The Basis of Nadia Boulanger's Teaching

In one of her very earliest published writings – the criticism of a performance of Mendelssohn's Italian Symphony early in 1919 – she went into very precise and very practical details about the entries of the various groups of instruments, the way in which the players neglected to watch the conductor, and the way in which the proper note values were observed or rather were not observed. But all of this was said with no hint of malice, simply a cool and practical look at what was happening, with some very practical observations as to what might be done to improve things.

Of course she knew that there were great problems of finance and administration to overcome. There was rarely enough time to rehearse properly, and players substituted for each other to such a degree that conductors might not see the same players in front of them at consecutive rehearsals. Even when it came to the performance, there was often considerable change in personnel if players had received offers of a more lucrative engagement that evening – a practice that still dogs some orchestras.

Shortly after World War Two the Boyd Neel orchestra went to give a concert in Paris, and, in reviewing the performance, Nadia Boulanger revealed her criteria for ideal conditions in conducting, and how near the Boyd Neel concert had come to them. The privilege of the Boyd Neel Orchestra, in her estimation, was that it 'loved order' to the point of turning it into a pleasure, and making it sensitive and natural. Of course this is entirely consistent with Nadia Boulanger's whole philosophy of music, that technique is mastered to the point where it sets the performer free to interpret the essentials of the music. Boyd Neel himself gave the impression that he had really little to do but stand there and let the orchestra play. In fact, as Nadia Boulanger pointed out, this was simply an impression. If one looked closely, one could see that there was a constant communication between players and conductor, and that the former carried out what the latter very clearly and precisely indicated. She also felt that they had had plenty of rehearsal time, so that the works on the programme were properly prepared and ready for performance, with the result that the concert was a joy.

Her own experience has made her fully aware of all the problems, so she does not speak in theoretical terms about conducting. She knows all the drawbacks, the pitfalls and the temptations. While praising the young Pierre Dervaux, as he was in 1946, for his authority and intelligence, she nevertheless warned him against the pleasure to be gained from captivating the audience. She recognized that he had the power to do so, but that the temptation was, in her opinion, fatal, and there were plenty of historical examples to prove the point. One might easily overstep the mark. Gestures that ought to be restrained could become an end in themselves and then, worst of all, the public no longer listens to the music but watches the conductor.

In a very early review of a concert conducted by Gabriel Pierné, whose musicianship and whole approach to his profession were those with which Nadia Boulanger had a great deal of sympathy, she quoted some words that André Suarès (1868–1948) originally applied to Wagner, but which expressed her view of the role and nature of the conductor:

'The great conductor is always a despot by temperament and intractable in his ways. Few arts demand and develop the will more . . . Few occupations put to the test one's patience, one's mastery of oneself and one's will more. The artist is obliged to keep his laughter and his tears to himself. If they want to emerge, in spite of himself, then he must hide them, or unleash them in someone else.'

In the last resort, however despotic a conductor might be, the creation of a musical experience requires the cooperation of three parties – the composer, the conductor and his co-interpreters, and the listener. If any one of these three fails to cooperate with the others, the performance no longer exists. The magic cannot work.

8

Nadia Boulanger's Musical Philosophy

From 15 December 1918 Nadia Boulanger undertook to write the notices of the Colonne-Lamoureux concerts in the musical magazine *Le Monde Musical*. In fact her first article did not appear until the issue for January 1919, and she did not contribute a great many of them. Also, she soon restricted herself to the Concerts Colonne. However, we are extremely fortunate in having these articles, since they contain her philosophy of music, which has hardly changed, except possibly to become even more profound, over the rest of her career.

What is remarkable is that after almost sixty years, in the course of which she has become naturally more learned, she is noticeably less forthright in her views. Towards the end of 1973 she said, in response to an interviewer's question: 'You believe I am a prophet. I feel that you ask me things that if I could answer then the whole world would come to hear me talk, so I don't know at all. I have my poor little ways of thinking about this subject, but very timidly, very shyly, it's too above me, you see.'

The point is that for many she is indeed some sort of prophet, and people from all over the world come to hear her talk. For them she has charisma, not simply because she is Nadia Boulanger the legend, but because she has been given and still gives something practical, positive and life-enhancing, and will do so until she dies. Some of those early articles seem to have something to say that is even more relevant half a century later, because certain tendencies that she saw then have become even more pronounced, and in some cases mankind has already succumbed to them. The quality of the writing, and its clarity, are as one might expect from a person of her calibre, and yet perhaps surprising in someone who was not trained or even particularly experienced as a writer.

In the last article that she wrote for the year 1919 she made a calmly intense statement of her intent:

'It is rarely a question of emotion in the course of these articles, and yet all the same the passionate love of music and the hope of propagating it, respect for life, for its sweetnesses and its sufferings, dictate them from the first to the last line. But in order to reach that goal, imagine what sort of words one would have to use. I have read some excellent ones, and I have heard admirable ones – how should I dare write others? And then is it not understood that at the origin of our conversations is the religion of music. As Mauclair has said: "One does not learn to love, but one learns to understand that which one loves."'

This basic conception of the role of music is fundamental to Nadia Boulanger's method of teaching, as well as to her philosophy of music. It is developed and referred to in her writing for *Le Monde Musical* in the May issue for 1919:

'Nothing is better than music; when it takes us out of time, it has done more for us than we have the right to hope for: it has broadened the limits of our sorrowful life, it has lit up the sweetness of our hours of happiness by effacing the pettinesses that diminish us, bringing us back pure and new to what was, what will be, what music has created for us.

'In music everything is prolonged, everything is edified, and when the enchantment has ceased, we are still bathed in its clarity; solitude is accompanied by a new hope between pity for ourselves – which makes us more indulgent and more understanding – and the certitude of finding something again, that which lives for ever in music.'

Such a heightened concept of the role of music, which assumes almost a moral quality, naturally has implications for those who exercise it as a profession. It is a difficult discipline to follow at the best of times, but becomes even more so with such ideals. It is consequently all the more easy to dismiss it as pious nonsense, as indeed some have done. And yet what Nadia Boulanger wrote over fifty years ago seems even more apposite at the present time: 'But – and from this stems so much bitterness and lost happiness – each human being wants to "lead his own life", to draw towards himself all the forces that he deems necessary for his fulfilment or his consolation, and heaps up on himself; lost in theories that conceal his own fierce and narrow egotism from him, he no longer sees the happiness he possesses, dreaming of the impossible.' Such sentiments are not fashionable in today's engulfing tide of materialism.

'And this conception of the individual for the individual is one of the greatest moral and artistic errors, a deep-seated cause of imbalance and negation. Technically the practical element kills the vital element, when it is taken as a pretext instead of being taken as expression.

'The force of analysis, the facility for writing, originality itself, as necessary as they are, become detrimental when they are put in the foreground, since the point of departure and the final result ought to be one and the same, without anything breaking the logic that demands that the *means* express the *music*, and not that the *music* expresses the *means*.'

The whole question of 'content' versus technical facility is a very vexed one. Once the Romantic concept of the artist as a passionate soul burning with inspiration gained currency – and in this respect the artists themselves at times seemed to encourage this view as much as anyone else – facility and pure technical ability came to be decried as unworthy of high art. At that very moment, however, these two elements were virtually all that was left, for it seems now that many of the great Romantics managed to say little superbly well, and at great length.

As we enter the last quarter of the twentieth century, the wheel may, in some way, be said to have come full circle, since many of the more avant-garde composers seem to minimize the content or element of inspiration in their work. Indeed, when presented with music that leaves so much to the whims of the performers, as in aleatoric music, it is hard to see how much such a composition may truly be regarded as a work of a composer in the traditional sense. One must exclude such a composer as Pierre Boulez from this category, however, because he cares very much about the way his music is performed. Boulez' experiences as a conductor have strengthened his other assets, namely a brilliant musical mind and an excellent ear.

It is interesting that Nadia Boulanger should have written over fifty years ago about this conflict, especially since she was reared in an age when the Romantic concept was still very much in vogue, as indeed it still is among many who go to concerts. Musical Paris of 1919 was much more in sympathy with the previous *artistic* century than the present one. Now that we are further removed by almost another century, we can once more appreciate the technical skill of the Romantic artists, and accept what they had to offer on its own terms. Moreover we are now seeing a surge of nostalgia for these more familiar modes of expression in an environment that is becoming increasingly more alien and uncongenial to us.

Yet we cannot and must not deny the present. Time and time again Nadia Boulanger comes back to this. To live only in the past is to deny that anything can survive from our age. But to live solely in the present is, in her opinion, equally dangerous:

> 'If we put from us the works of the Past, and deny ourselves the emotions they diffuse, we are in fact denying the possibility of survival to contemporary art.
>
> 'If we diminish their power, we diminish that of art in general, for nothing could be reborn from the destruction. But to stop dead so as only to contemplate what has been is just as great a mistake.
>
> 'Now, two opposite phenomena occur: either an exaggerated tendency to look upon our own epoch as decadent; or a propensity – no less exaggerated – to consider as worthwhile only that which is being produced at the present time. The infinite variety in life dominates these anxieties, and gives each event more real greatness and less exterior importance. That which is sincere, that which is beautiful, does not become petrified.'

To have the critical acumen and the culture to live on such a plane, and treat music of past, present and future with equanimity, requires something of a tightrope performer's skill that very few are capable of performing. What, then, are her criteria for the music that she would accept and encourage? As one might expect, she starts from basic principles. In December 1919 she wrote: 'Music is made of two essential elements (line and rhythm), which are complemented by decorative elements (harmony and orchestration) – the goal is achieved if the co-ordinated use of these elements corresponds to the emotion from which is born the idea that they are intended to develop.' In other words, music is basically an emotion, which gives birth to an idea. To express the idea – and ultimately the emotion, by extension – the technique of the musician is brought into operation. In fact this approach may embrace both the Romantic concept of inspiration and the craftsman-composer who may write a work to a specific commission. If the emotion is there, it will become an idea, and the technique will translate the idea into music.

Despite the great role that music has to play in the life of man, it is essentially something one may approach with practicality, as a business, in fact, and the business of making music has certain implicit demands for performers and listeners alike:

'We usually know one of the *métiers* of music, and we know the individual technicalities of it – but what about its soul, its fundamental laws? We listen, we applaud or we are bored . . . and without going any further we go on our way. The day when we have to perform we set about work in detail, carried along by the inspiration of the moment and . . . the adventure unfolds itself, outside our real consciousness.

'The concert ought in the first place to be a source of emotion for us, but in the second a source of study, of progress. One ought to prepare for it, and one ought to benefit from it. Nothing happens without reason, it is simply that the reasons sometimes remain unintelligible to us, because we do not see very far, because we do not take the trouble to look, but they surely exist.'

In this one is reminded very much of the ideas of Benjamin Britten, who feels that listeners should take much more trouble with their concertgoing. He feels that music should be much more of an occasion. People should save up to go, and study the music if possible beforehand. By implication, therefore, some people go to too many concerts, or go there too easily. For all the benefits that they bring, the radio and gramophone in this context may well have an unfortunate effect. We may have music at the touch of a switch, whereas each hearing should be a unique occasion. We need to prepare ourselves for it. As Nadia Boulanger has written: 'In order to listen to music, one must be neither sentimental nor hostile; in order to judge it one must feel revolt, impartiality or confidence; in order to love it, one must either be emotional to the point of recognizing Beauty whatever its mode of expression, or educated to the point of recognizing the governing thought, whatever period it is expressed in.'

There are obligations for the performers, too, however. Here is Nadia Boulanger once more: 'As far as the execution is concerned . . . one might say that the most frequent and most serious mistake is to follow the music instead of preceding it.' Here she was thinking especially of a sense of rhythm, which she feels is so deficient in many people, but also in a wider sense of always being in the wake of musical developments, rather than out in front. However, she was well aware that new music created problems for listeners:

> 'Why is the public – reasonably well informed and clearsighted when it comes to the past – so distrustful or credulous, so wary or careless when it is a question of new works?
>
> 'There are several causes.
>
> 'Materially there are not sufficient means of penetration, not enough repeat performances.
>
> 'To understand, one must assimilate the language to the point where one no longer needs to worry about the words; one needs to know the mind, and familiarize oneself with the ambiance.'

Obviously this is asking a great deal of the average concert-goer, even today; and as for performers, it is a big step for them to concentrate on contemporary music, as they have to if they are going to perform it adequately. The rewards are usually small financially, and whether or not they are small artistically, too, depends on the temperament of the performer. At all events music is an exacting discipline, as Nadia Boulanger pointed out, whether one delves deep into contemporary music or not. All music demands devotion and application, and even more than that, for brilliance without understanding is, in her eyes, useless.

She has never been a lover of showmanship for its own sake: 'With their shining intelligence, they must make extravagances – a need, showing that something is not at peace – a moment of defeat, of sadness – I do not find it original.' Or even more succinctly: 'To be a composer and not a musician is a tragedy; it is to have genius and not talent.'

As a teacher this is important to Nadia Boulanger, because

not all her pupils have been born geniuses. She admits that geniuses do exist, of course, and that some of them need little technical assistance. 'If you are a genius who knows nothing, learns nothing and can write masterpieces, good, it is a mystery of God. And I believe in miracles. And so it's very simple; so is a miracle, and many masterpieces are unbelievable miracles. And we know that very well, as a gift is a miracle. But you cannot prepare people for a miracle.' In other words, if a person is not a genius, then he needs to be equipped. 'You must give them the way to fight, and to fight is only to have a technique.'

The technique is only a means to an end, however, because pure facility in technique – whether it be in writing music or as a performer – is only a stage along the road to the unveiling of the music itself:

'You have a number of people who are instrumental in a purely mechanical way. And they may become what one is obliged to call virtuosi. They can play very accurately, very fast, but they convey nothing because at heart there is no contact with the work itself, with the meaning and what it actually is. To me the greatest objective is when the composer disappears, the performer disappears, and there remains only the work – but that you can do only with great masterpieces. They stand by themselves, only by themselves.

'To be more precise: one plays the notes as one reads them, the same way as one notes the immediate relationship of their respective values – discovering the horizon step by step – it is obviously easier, but what becomes of the tune and the rhythm then?'

In Nadia Boulanger's view we need to have a comprehensive view of a piece of music, a complete understanding of it. All too often, in her estimation, and this was especially true in earlier days, this rarely happens. Whether a work is short or long, it has a beginning and an end. It is the task of the performer, through analysis and intuition, to decide on the general shape of the piece in relation to its proportions, which are dictated by two fixed points, the beginning and the end. Even when one is sight reading, one must try to give complete pictures, because incomplete ones do not convey, or allow the listener to form, a conception of the ensemble. 'A poor but faithful reproduction of a work of art explains it better to us than the original work revealed in fragments.'

What Nadia Boulanger was advocating in the early articles,

and has continued to advocate throughout her life, is a deeper understanding, a more informed understanding, so that appreciation will be enhanced. As she pointed out, even the most audacious composers, from Beethoven to Schumann, Berlioz and Wagner, were interested in what had gone before. 'So as to understand the modernism that each period always carries in itself, in relation to what has gone before, one must initiate oneself into its means of expression, into the general atmosphere: we scarcely linger over it any more, and it is a great pity. It was such a good training for the mind to discipline itself before setting itself free . . . We know the names of an enormous number of things, but is that enough?'

At that time Nadia Boulanger could scarcely have known that it would have implications for herself, and that with the advent of dodecaphony she would have to come to terms with what were to her alien concepts in music. It is much to her credit, whatever some critics have said, that she showed herself willing to do so. Even pupils who discovered that they no longer spoke the same musical language admit that she was prepared to try and converse with them. She felt that she was living in such a climate in 1919:

'Now, we are going through an unprecedented period of transition, following the Wagnerian domination, a period that is perhaps so defined, so rich, because the willingly accepted yoke was so imperious.

'The vocabulary is therefore of necessity new, since the great creative souls are expressing a new state of mind; since they open our eyes to new visions, and since the artists who live in their effulgence use it as they do and, in these circumstances, abundance and originality are themselves part of the trouble we endure.'

Supporting her, however, was her vision of continuity, which enabled her to connect everything in a chain of being:

'In fact, certain unalterable feelings, impressions that are forever renewed, have been translated across the ages, in periods which had their respective progressions, paroxysms, and their decline. These periods link up with each other and are superimposed in such a way that each paroxysm brings a new progression, and each decline sees an apogee.

'Thus art is indeed the synthesis of life.'

It is here that one reaches the kernel of Nadia Boulanger's thought, a thought that she has expressed throughout her life, and in her life itself.

'Now, if genius consists in understanding the Past and expressing the Future, whilst existing in the Present, every work of art remains modern in respect of its period, and ought to remain so for us, in the highest sense of the word. One may therefore risk the most remote juxtapositions in a programme without accident, on condition that one always observes the rule of movement that requires a direction, some logic.'

This brought her to the conclusion that it was essential for the composer to possess ideas capable of synthesis, while for performers the prime objective should be an idea of the ensemble – as she described it, 'a non-visual development in space, fugitive in time, forcing music to express itself in great authority and style.'

In such a theory, genius may be defined:

'The artist who dominates his period synthesizes it during its progress, either as a whole – and then it is like the gift of prophecy – or under one of its manifestations, which explains the simultaneous existence of geniuses so opposed to one another. When each one is anxious in the face of his interior confusion, when each event is an enigma which seems to increase the obscurity, a predestined artist comes and takes over our most mysterious and most hidden being. Whether consciously or not, he extracts from all the struggling, all the confusion, all the contradictions, the essential thought which will eventually give a style to the whole of a period, which will distinguish it and will ensure him a place in the eternal sphere.

'One is bound to be uneasy in the face of such prescience.

'And this brings us back to our point of departure: neither sentimentality nor hostility, but revolt, impartiality or confidence because, over and above what constitutes an insult to art by its very essence, and which we are not concerned with here, present-day works that live off the past are abnormal; those which only know the present, or fashion, are useless; whilst the only true ones are those which lead us on further, since they alone are creating life.

'May all of our impassioned heart go to them for they are the ones that, from time immemorial, have constituted the light in the shadows, the ideal in the midst of materialism.'

Of course all this was written before the dodecaphonic school developed and all the various subsequent experimentations took place. Nadia Boulanger has tried to live up to the lofty ideals she set herself, namely accepting everything insofar as it has its place in the history of musical development, but there had to come a point beyond which she simply could not go.

For her, humanity must remain the linchpin in music, but the tendency of most contemporary serious music has been depersonalization, and one is led to conclude that the end product of this will be silence – the total rejection of personality. At the other end of the scale, a vast industry has grown up to provide music at a debased popular level. This is not, however, a genuine popular culture, because it has not emerged out of the people, it has been imposed upon them.

The English music critic and composer Wilfrid Mellers, in the final essay entitled 'Music and Society Now', which he contributed to *Music and Western Man*, sums up the predicament of the twentieth-century composer very succinctly, and although he was writing some twenty years ago, his words are even more true today. 'Serious' music has split into two apparently irreconcilable camps, while 'Pop' music has degenerated into amplified cacophony. As Mellers wrote:

> 'The twentieth-century composer's position is unprecedented in the sense that he is willy-nilly a parasite. A real musical culture should not be a museum culture based mainly on the music of past ages; nor should it be, like most commercial music, a drug. It should be the active embodiment in sound of the life of a community – of the everyday demands of people's work and play and of their deepest spiritual needs. Clearly, a more creative conception of musical culture can come only with a more creative society.'

For Nadia Boulanger a non-creative society is virtually inconceivable. The rest of us despair and at the same time live in hope.

9

The Uniqueness of Nadia Boulanger

As a person Nadia Boulanger can be a variety of things – generous, kind, even affectionate. She is also capable of being very entertaining, and she must have one of the largest numbers of imitators in the world. When she is talking seriously, there is a quality about her delivery that gives added weight to her words. Even when writing, one can almost hear her speaking them: 'More often than not we talk about things that we scarcely know, we often discuss things of which we have no knowledge, and in reality we are ignorant of that which we think we love.'

Her use of language has always been most illuminating, whether written or spoken. She writes elegant French, as one might expect, and even in her declining years speaks beautifully. Her English has always had a touch of the picturesque. She wrote to Gustav Holst in 1929, apologizing for being 'awkward in French, paralysed in English'. Doubtless her wartime stay in America helped to improve her English, but even as late as 1967, when taking master classes in London, she was still apologetic. 'I would be more at ease if I had more words.' She also apologized for having 'no Latin, no Greek – a hole in the mind one cannot fill up'.

From a teaching point of view, of course, an unusual combination of words often helps to fix something in the pupil's mind much more securely than does everyday language, since powers of association are particularly strong in learning. This has been especially true in Nadia Boulanger's case, since former students almost always break into a French vaudeville accent when imitating her, and reproduce her choice of words most faithfully. If nothing else, this is a tribute to her persona.

The title chosen for a BBC programme in September 1973, when she was eighty-six, was 'The Tender Tyrant'. It was a very concise and astute summing-up of the nature of this extraordinary person. Tender she doubtless is towards many, since she is surrounded by a group of friends who would almost, one suspects, be prepared to die for her. Yet these same people seem to live in fear of her, almost as if she were some sort of tyrant, and they are not even privy to some of her important decisions – for example, concerning the disposal of her papers on her death. No one knows whether they are to be a bequest to the nation to be deposited in the Bibliothèque Nationale, or form the nucleus of a Lili Boulanger Foundation or institute. Her letters to them are private, and they would not make them public for anything in the world – through a mixture of deep affection and, one suspects, a certain element of fear. One can only respect these feelings.

The term Tender Tyrant also has a much wider application, for it admirably covers her dealings with the musical world at large. She has rarely denounced or condemned in public, but on the few occasions when she has, she has done it without hysteria, on the one hand, or without mincing her words or attempting to soften the blow, on the other. By way of contrast, when *Ol-Ol*, an opera by her friend the Russian composer Alexander Tcherepnin, was given on the radio in France, she wrote to him to thank him the next day, despite the fact that at that time she could hardly see the paper on which she wrote. Such gestures matter a great deal to her, and they are not done merely as a matter of form – she is much too busy for that – but as a spontaneous action expressing her pleasure both at the music and at the success of a friend and colleague.

It is in relation to her teaching that the sobriquet 'Tender Tyrant' really has most application. With many students the tender tyranny has been one that they have been very happy to accept, and it has caused them no pains. One such was the American composer Roy Harris, who enjoyed a particularly good relationship with Nadia Boulanger.

Roy Harris went to France in 1926, at the age of twenty-eight. At first he lived by the Seine at Chatou, but the combination of the dampness that winter and his wife – described by

Virgil Thomson as a 'worried reader of intellectual magazines'
– were not conducive to his composition. He abandoned both
Chatou and wife, and went to live near Gargenville, where
Nadia Boulanger spent a lot of time in those days. The new
location suited both Roy Harris and his music, and he got on
well with his teacher. In fact he taught her how to drive a car,
and in return she decided to try and find him a new wife – this
time someone who would be able to help him with his music
and, if possible, financially as well. He almost fell in with this
scheme, but in the end settled for a young woman who was
happy to help him with his music, and not so concerned about
matrimony.

Every now and then Nadia Boulanger had this sort of relation with a pupil, though naturally as she grew older, and her
pupils, by comparison, grew progressively younger, relations
tended to move away from these lines. Even so, she has always
had a flair for finding the right tone for any given relationship;
and without ever compromising herself, giving any suggestion
of talking down to a less gifted person or, for that matter, being
obsequious to the grand, she relates in a direct and interested
manner to virtually everyone she meets.

Moreover she remembers people with alarming precision.
When meeting one of her former pupils, a singer, after a break
of some years in communication, she quite unnerved her by
saying, 'You know, my dear, you are extremely lucky to have
such a great gift of a beautiful voice.' Even if one cynically assumes that she had been prompted to inform herself about the
singer in advance, she at least deserves the credit for having
taken the trouble to do so.

What Roy Harris most valued was what he saw as two apparently contradictory strands in Nadia Boulanger's make-up,
namely the idealist in her that longed for a world in which
music would lead mankind into a better way of life, or at all
events enrich that way of life considerably, and the realist in her
that saw the obstacles and the probable pitfalls, but who nevertheless was determined to overcome them. He appreciated her
concern for the welfare of her students, but at the same time he
saw that she could also be stern and just in her appraisal of their
abilities and achievements. In his own words: 'Of such ideal-
ism, tempered by such realism, is the structure of greatness

created.' There are many who would agree with him in this.

It was Roy Harris who, in 1973, recalled the shrewd way in which Nadia Boulanger planned her teaching routine in the early days, a plan that has more or less persisted to the present time:

> 'Everyone knows where he or she stands in the Boulanger order of importance. At any given time, the least developed are assigned to Mondays, moreover the least of these just come Monday mornings. Tuesday students are a step forward. If you are a Wednesday, everyone knows you are a borderline case who might graduate to Thursday. Friday's students have promise, and prospective [*sic*]. They are expected to stay for Nadia's famous Friday afternoon teas, where sooner or later all musical celebrities gravitate. Saturday's students – few indeed – are the cream of the craft. Only one obvious standout ever makes it for Saturday night dinner followed by intoxicating hours of intense musical considerations and opinions.'

This teaching, even now, may start at eight o'clock in the morning, with Nadia Boulanger sometimes not even stopping for lunch but eating while she continues a lesson, and it might go on until half past one in the morning. When she does relax properly, however, then, as one might expect, she throws herself into it with zest. She loves parties, which is possibly a legacy from her Russian mother. She enjoys people and food, and elegant occasions. But when it is time for work again, she devotes herself to it with – in Yehudi Menuhin's words – the commitment of an ant with the dedication of a saint.

Yehudi Menuhin sees a lot of similarities between her and his own mother, who was Russian, and several of the elements in her make-up, particularly her belief in a band of elect and her nostalgia, he sees as legacies from the Russian character. Menuhin first met her at the age of eleven, when he sat next to her at a banquet to celebrate a musical occasion. He had just been given the *Gesellschaft* edition of the Bach solo violin sonatas by his father, and he and Nadia Boulanger spent a long time discussing them. They have remained friends ever since. She often stays at his house in London, where her shoes are made to order – one of the few luxuries she permits herself, along with her black evening gowns from Lanvin. He confesses himself at a loss to imagine what can be in the five or six suitcases she always brings with her, since she only wears white and black or grey. Presumably all the things that are most precious to her travel with her, but that is essentially her own private realm.

It is not surprising that someone who has led such a public life for so long should have a private realm into which she can withdraw if need be, and where certain personal thoughts, even secrets, may be kept. It is not a particularly fashionable thing to do at the present time, but Nadia Boulanger has never been particularly worried about fashion. Evolution is a different matter, but then, as she wisely pointed out many years ago, the problem for most people is how to distinguish between fashion and evolution. Subject as we are to saturation by news media and advertising, there seems to be an automatic assumption that the sort of progress we are making at the present time is unquestionably good, and therefore to be pursued. We could do a lot worse than quote some words she wrote in April 1919: 'There are old things and new things that we must love and defend, as there are old things and new things that we must oppose. Let us therefore only consider our conscience, without worrying ourselves unduly about the judgements that the direction of our conscience will bring down upon us.'

Not everyone is gifted with such clarity of vision, or such integrity, when it comes to making a decision and sticking to it. In teaching, of course, making the right decision is crucial. If a teacher is trying to guide a pupil into one particular path, or dissuade him from one he may already have chosen, the teacher must be sure that what he is doing is the right course of action for that particular pupil. He must be very sure of his conscience, especially if he is going to assume the role of a tyrant. If he and the pupil see eye to eye with one another, there will be no tyranny and much tenderness, one hopes; and Nadia Boulanger has enjoyed notably tender relations with many of her pupils.

The reverse of this particular aspect of the student-teacher relationship is the tyranny that goes along with the tenderness. Many of Nadia Boulanger's most fervent admirers and former pupils admit *en passant* to a streak of cruelty in her. Amid terms of affection and admiration the word is almost overlooked, and it is only afterwards that the implications are fully realized. Hugo Cole, for example, said that she could be cruel to casual or uncommitted students, and that she made no allowance for fatigue or timidity: 'Sleepers in the dormitory are nice – when one makes music the function is to keep awake.' This is of course consistent with the beliefs she has always made quite plain, that if one chooses to do something, then one must do it supremely well.

It is not only to the uncommitted that she is capable of being cruel. There have been students who have persevered with her because they felt that she had something to offer them, and they were still, in their estimation, treated badly. Naturally she would not see it at all in those terms, and one can only look at the evidence as dispassionately as possible. A case in point is that of the distinguished American composer David Diamond.

In the summer of 1936 Diamond went to Paris while he was working on his ballet *Tom* and his String Quartet Concerto. He went to see Nadia Boulanger, who invited him to go to the American Conservatory at Fontainebleau that summer. He declined, however, because he did not want to interrupt his work in Paris, and Fontainebleau is not especially convenient, even with today's improved communications, if one is based on central Paris. Next spring, however, Nadia Boulanger was in New York, staying at an apartment on Park Avenue, where she invited David Diamond to come and see her. He had been working at a drugstore soda counter and had damaged his right hand, so was unable to play anything for her, but he took along the score of his Psalm for Orchestra, with which she was impressed, and she seemed delighted with the possibility of working together. She said that both Aaron Copland and Koussevitsky had spoken well of him, and that she would get a scholarship for him, which she did. A ticket arrived from the New York office of the American Conservatory at Fointainebleau, and so he left America to spend the summer of 1937 in France.

It was only when it was time to return after the summer session that David Diamond looked at his ticket and discovered that there was no return section. Nadia Boulanger declined any responsibility for this, maintaining that it was the responsibility of the New York office. They, however, replied that no return passage was guaranteed. In the event two friends put up the money for him, and he was able to return as planned. Before he left, he telephoned Nadia Boulanger to tell her that he had been able to make arrangements for his return, and that he was not angry, only hurt. To this she replied that it would not be the only time in his life that he would be hurt. The mistake about the ticket had originated in New York, she continued, but she bore him no hard feelings, and wished him well. She said that he was too sensitive, and that he would pay a hard price for it. However, communications were not severed, since she said that they would talk the next time she was in the States.

Obviously this was a very anxious time for David Diamond. He had been working on his Flute Quintet, which was commissioned by the League of Composers, and there had been differences with Nadia Boulanger during its composition. The commission fee was $200, of which only $100 was sent as an advance, and then the blow of the one-way ticket fell. The composer eventually developed a chronic case of giant urticaria and related skin trouble, but from the outset Nadia Boulanger had never appeared to feel any responsibility in the matter. David Diamond felt that since she had been so keen for him to go and study with her, there was at least a moral obligation for her to try and help him, and it was probably within her power to do so, not necessarily out of her private funds, but by exercising pressure on those officials able to do so.

After such glowing tributes from other students whom she did help in a very practical way, why did this happen? The relation between pupil and teacher is always a potentially complicated one, particularly with a student who has progressed beyond the schoolroom; and that between a male pupil and female teacher is especially delicate. Whether consciously or not, they confront each other with a combination of any or all of the possible relationships between a man and a woman, so that in addition to that of teacher and pupil, there are shades of mother and son, husband and wife, and lover and mistress; and it is usually only when the teacher and the pupil fail to see eye to eye that the nuances become apparent. When artistic temperaments come into it also, the mixture is latently explosive.

What, in the circumstances, is a teacher to do? In Nadia Boulanger's mind she was no doubt remaining true to herself and her principles. If a pupil came to her, she might modify her methods, but not the content of her instruction. In David Diamond's case it was perhaps unfortunate for him that, in spite of his first experience, he still felt fascinated by her, and that she had much to offer him. Consequently, when he received his first Guggenheim Fellowship, he decided to return to Paris for a year, starting in the spring of 1938, to work both as a private pupil and at Fontainebleau in the summer of that year.

This time the tenor of the working relationship was much calmer, but it was still very difficult for David Diamond to accept certain things: for example, what he saw as the praising of mediocre talents, the small and insensitive cruelties to certain students, and the discouraging of such enthusiasms of his as the Bartók quartets (of which only five had been written then), and the music of Satie, Schönberg and Webern. If he brought any of the scores to lessons, she would take them and place them on her second piano in the salon and return to the first piano, at which the lesson was to be conducted. He saw his year of work as one of little encouragement but much criticism, and drew little solace from his supposed resemblance to Watteau faces, or comments on his over-sensitivity and strong resentments. It did not improve matters when he remarked that his teacher also had strong resentments.

Unfortunately that was not to be the end of the affair. David Diamond had been in Paris for the première of Stravinsky's *Agon* in October 1957. On entering the Salle Pleyel he walked straight into Nadia Boulanger's box, where she was talking to Yvonne de Casa Fuerte. She broke off the conversation and took the hand he offered her, and apologized for not having seen him when she was last in Florence. However, there was to be a party the following evening given by Nicolas Nabokov, where Nadia would talk with David and make an appointment to meet. At that point, David Diamond had not actually been invited to the Nabokov party, but after the concert he met Stravinsky, Boulez and Nabokov in the street, and was automatically invited.

When it came to the party, however, Nadia Boulanger always managed to avoid David Diamond, and when he smiled at her across the room, she looked at him as if she did not know him. After an evening of this he became successively perplexed, depressed and finally furious, and determined to approach Nadia and calmly tell her that that was not the way to treat people.

He then returned to Florence, and wrote to her about the incident, whereupon she replied, in English:

'If I were the one you picture, your letter would offend me – but, it only renders me very sad, for it shows how unhappy you are. Don't believe I am cross – I am not, and will not try to explain anything. What good could result? What I want only to say is that your letter changes nothing. What you say about 1937 I don't understand either.

'I do hope you will find in yourself peace and perhaps realize what you tried to do, fortunately in vain. Why only, if your feeling became so bitter and despising did you write so affectionately.

'Well, all that will take its right place. I have the same feelings which an agressif [*sic*] letter cannot touch and I wish you what you wish yourself – above all peace at heart.'

In the circumstances one probably could not have expected any different a reply. In her own mind she had done nothing to warrant such an attack as David Diamond's action at the party and his subsequent letter had constituted. It was therefore a relatively simple course for her to take – she forgave him, and observed that if she was such a dreadful person as all that, why had he written in such affectionate terms?

That, of course, is only half the matter. Once we are aware of the affections of another person towards us, however, and we tacitly accept them, then a relationship exists, for better or for worse, and extricating oneself is inevitably a painful business.

Some people attract others to them almost whether they like it or not, and in this case they can be absolved from any responsibility towards the would-be adherents. A teacher is a different matter entirely, since by his or her very nature pupils are encouraged to come and lay bare their inmost being, to be subjected to the most rigorous scrutiny. As Nadia Boulanger said in an interview:

'Really, you know, you can't develop or change anything in anybody. You can respect what he is and try to make him a true picture of himself. As a teacher, my whole life is based on understanding the others, not on making them understand me. What the student thinks, what he wants to do – that is the important thing. I must try to make him express himself and prepare him to do that for which he is best fitted.'

But what if she does understand the student, and cannot come to terms with what is there? As she said in a much more recent interview:

> '. . . each student must have an opinion, must know how he would like to play, and then you can permit yourself to say "I think you are wrong, it seems to me that you don't hear well." But how can you, as far as interpretation or composition is concerned, how can you be sure of what you say? You can be sure that you are honest, that you are convinced and you give the reason for your conviction, that you believe this conviction represents a truth.'

Yet, as is obviously implicit in the foregoing, there is always the possibility that the teacher may be wrong, and that a budding musician may be maimed for life. To avert such a tragedy, a teacher may always say to his pupil that he can do nothing for him. Unfortunately not many seem to do this, and so events move inexorably to a breakdown. When the teacher-pupil relation has been complicated by emotional attachment – be it only one of loyalty on the part of the student – then the result can only be an unhappy one.

The English composer Nicholas Maw, who went to Nadia Boulanger on the advice of Lennox Berkeley, always felt that his relation with her was of an equivocal nature. He could never quite make up his mind whether she approved of him or not. When he was a student, however, she was both kind and generous to him, which made it all the more difficult for him, on reflection, to express reservations about some of the demands she makes on her students, and some of her teaching methods. In fact he was a recipient of a Lili Boulanger Memorial Fund Award in 1959, but initially his lessons did not start on a very good footing. Eventually, however, they agreed to bury their differences, and afterwards she always treated him with great friendliness and consideration.

In the last resort, however, he felt that he learnt more about French and European culture in general, and about life, from Nadia Boulanger, than he learnt about music. Fortunately he was able to evaluate this and accept it, and pass on. In no way did he feel his time had been wasted, and he freely admits that Nadia Boulanger is one of the most commanding figures in twentieth-century music.

The Uniqueness of Nadia Boulanger

There may have been many more failures than have been made public, and in an attempt to look at both sides of the question one has to be careful not to exaggerate the failures at the expense of the successes. We live in an age when in our efforts to be fair to all parties we almost lose sight of the norm. In the last resort one cannot seek to apportion blame or approbation, one can simply present as much of the evidence as one can assemble, in as objective a manner as possible, because ultimately the matter is resolved in the consciences of the individuals concerned.

It would seem that Nadia Boulanger and her conscience have been at one with each other for some time past, and that she for one is quite prepared for any judgements she might bring down upon herself. And indeed, when one directs one's gaze outwards, the *summum* of her life and work receives wholehearted support. Her vision of man's purpose in this life, and of the specific role of music in it, must surely win the approval of virtually any musician and music-lover, or, for that matter, anyone at all concerned with and for man's destiny. She has the elevated vision of life that we need today even more urgently than when she first formulated it over fifty years ago.

Writing in January 1920, Nadia Boulanger began by surveying the chronological extent of the works performed in the public concerts being given in Paris; and this led her on to a consideration of music and life that brought her to the conclusion that the two are almost synonymous, and almost interchangeable.

'If we consider the succession of works, the multiplicity of expression, the evolution of the process, we are struck by both the narrowness and the marvellous immensity of life.

'Always the same feelings, always the same suffering, the same love, always the need to push back the limit of the known, always this anxiety, because always something inside of us waits, without being able to define the nature of its waiting; always this vital force which, without ever ceasing, draws us along in the eternal movement, and also this aspiration to joy, to youth, to happiness in some abyss of distress, doubt or effort.

'In truth we have so little courage to live, and only see the days pass insofar as they bring us deception, without respect for what they show us that is great and, wasting ourselves in petty sensations of boredom, in regrets, in the fatigue of useless satisfactions, in the hope of illusory pleasures, we no longer see the unfolding of the incomparable spectacle which pits life against eternity.

'Men have passed at every epoch, fixing with their sadness and their joy, with their hearts and their brains, this tragic and magnificent struggle of mutual conquest, which is – from the most miserable to the most heroic – the common lot of human beings.

'These men – they were nothing else than each one of us, or almost so, in that they were heirs to the same misery, and yet put light where we do not even put shadows, through cowardice and impotence.

'We complain ceaselessly, not for suffering – suffering requires the silence in which memory and thought delight – but for not being fulfilled in what our love of self possesses that is most extrovert; for not resolving the chimerical problems created by our neurasthenic imaginations. Those who have lit up the road for eternity were always alone in the midst of the multitude, alone among loved ones, alone in seeing too high, too far, alone in some terrifying solitude, because the questions that reared up between them and the unknown are scarcely conceivable to us.

'Even so, it is through them, and only through them, that the life we are pleased to consider in its poverty and in its mediocrity, seems to us endlessly productive of emotions that are endlessly renewed, rich with unspeakable beauty, heavy with an unfathomable sorrow, truly great . . . and terrible and so beyond us, who see nothing.

'And for those who know how to listen, what a lesson. Those who are truly great – I mean in their music and in their soul, because the one may not be separated from the other and never is in fact, even when our judgement, paralysed by prejudices that are a "fashion" of the mind, makes us say that it is – those composers transpose all that they feel, and everything for them culminates in action. More often than not they retain the feeling of joy, the joy that is in the look of a loved one, in a flower, in the sky or in something that survives from the past, and when they know the ultimate sadness they transmute it into serenity.

'Words created divergencies between beings, because their precise meanings put an opinion around the idea. Music only retains the highest and purest substance of the idea, since it has the privilege of expressing all, whilst excluding nothing.'

Here then is the crux of the role that Nadia Boulanger sees music as playing, and which to a large extent she has played out in her own life and career. Because music speaks without imposing its opinion, or indeed offering any opinion at all, then it may truly speak to all men, no matter what their beliefs, and help them relate to the rest of humanity, and to all that man has experienced in the past and may yet experience in the future.

Of course this role is not restricted to music alone among the arts; she mentioned music because it was her particular domain. She has always had many artistic friends in addition to exclusively musical ones, and it is not surprising that she has always had a comprehensive view of the arts in relation to man, as she set forward in March 1920: 'The influence of the arts on each other is like a living circle around the need for the human being to expand, and when one ceases to inspire the other, a third comes and takes up the torch so that the ardent flame which is at the centre of life never goes out.'

Nadia Boulanger is indeed a unique phenomenon, and only in the fulness of time will we discover the exact extent of her influence. Without wishing to make the comparison appear odious, one may consider her career alongside that of another Frenchwoman who embarked on a musical career – Jeanne Leleu. She was born in 1898, entered the Conservatoire at the age of nine, studied with Marguerite Long, Chapuis, Caussade and Widor. In 1923 she won the Premier Grand Prix de Rome for musical composition. In 1947 she became professor in sight reading at the Conservatoire, and in 1952 professor of harmony, but her influence can in no way be said to match that of Nadia Boulanger.

Even the French, who seem to have ignored Nadia Boulanger for so long, at one moment awoke to the fact that there was something special about her and then almost as suddenly forgot her existence once more. One suspects, however, that if she had not been so well known abroad, this would not have happened. Music does not rank high in their priorities today, and it is not surprising to learn that until 1974 Orly airport, a now somewhat tarnished symbol of France's leap into the modern age, was the most popular national monument. One wonders whether the even newer Charles de Gaulle airport at Roissy will supplant Orly in French affections. If General de Gaulle remarked that it was impossible to govern a country that produced more than 300 cheeses, one might observe that it is equally impossible to bring culture to a nation whose chief delight is an airport.

A few years ago a series of gramophone records was made under the patronage of the Alliance Française, entitled *Français de notre temps*. Among the many famous names, Nadia Boulanger was number 83. To get her to talk at all was a triumph, and by way of introduction to the record, the secretary general of the Alliance Française, Marc Blancpain, wrote:

'For the people of my generation, Nadia Boulanger is "music". We were fifteen years old, with a fresh ear, a trembling heart and a totally fresh imagination, when she was attaining complete mastery and glory.

'Yes, one had to be, or have been, a pupil of Nadia Boulanger; or else, more modestly, it was indispensable to have heard such and such a disciple formed by her. It is to Nadia Boulanger, for a large part, that the French owe the loss of that annoying reputation – and at present unmerited – for being unmusical.

'Who then was more generous than she? Who then was able, like her, to disseminate knowledge, refine taste and form talent? As much in Paris as in London, in Rome and, directly or through the intermediary of the American Conservatory at Fontainebleau, throughout the New World.

'In order to prolong itself and develop, a civilization needs masters, creators and diffusers of light. French music, in this present century, has had no more shining master than Nadia Boulanger.'

The contents of the record make no startling revelations, but they typify the modesty, the sincerity, the wisdom and the humanity that are Nadia Boulanger. The claims of Marc. Blancpain that the French are no longer an unmusical nation, however, still ring somewhat hollow when one surveys the current scene; and the fact still remains that Nadia Boulanger has always been more appreciated outside France, or by foreigners rather than French people.

In trying to isolate the essential elements of her character for those who have not come into contact with her, or are unlikely to do so, possibly the most impressive quality that remains with one is her loyalty and devotion. In the first place, of course, this consists of devotion to her sister's memory, and the preservation and propagation of her music. Then to the memory of her teacher Fauré, of whose church music her fellow-pupil Charles

Koechlin recalled she once wrote: 'To have given this to our unhappy hearts, to have combined Charity with Beauty, Hope with Love, is not this the most beautiful mode of participating in the work of the Church?' She is loyal also to the memory of Stravinsky, and to her students – not only those who have made a name for themselves such as Aaron Copland, Jean Françaix or Lennox Berkeley and whose works she will use as illustrations in her teaching, but to those who might, at any time, be currently in her care.

Secondly there is her incredible determination or inner driving force, which has enabled her to do all that she has done virtually single-handed, and to demand so much of herself, well into her eighties. The sheer physical strain of teaching, travelling and relating to the hundreds of people she has encountered throughout her life, or even in the course of a single year, would have defeated a person of any lesser ability. One of the great supports in her own make-up to allow her to carry on at this pace has been her love of order and control. When one is young, one may underestimate this with impunity, but the value of it becomes apparent as the years advance. Of course it has the concomitant effect of a certain lack of adaptability, but this is a somewhat contemporary virtue, and may not always be at such a premium in the future as conditions in society evolve.

A third element, and closely related to the previous one, is her amazing, apparently inexhaustible, enthusiasm for almost everything around her. From this comes her ability to inspire enthusiasm in others, which has been of immense benefit not only in her teaching, but in her human relations. She is always eager for news of old friends or former pupils, and is capable of suddenly asking an assembled salon whether they know what has become of the Norwegian composer so-and-so, who studied with her some years ago.

Then one must always take account of her kindness and generosity to many people. We may never know just how far this extended, or in how many ways she helped the careers of friends and pupils.

There is a great temptation to try and be all things to all men, and a teacher is often required to do this without even wanting to. Where one must make a reservation in the case of Nadia Boulanger is the way she handled some people whose temperaments were not compatible with her own. It has been claimed, obviously with very good cause, that she was psychologically clever in her handling of her students. In this case the notable failures must also be regarded as failures as far as she is concerned. Or was it that her psychology was even more subtle than she was given credit for, and that by virtually provoking rupture she opened people's eyes for them?

From a purely musical point of view it is hard, in view of the current state of music, to attempt any precise estimation of the absolute value of the content of her teaching, or to envisage what sort of niche she will eventually occupy in the history of music. By any accounts the evidence to date must surely imply that her achievement will have been outstanding.

Index

Index

innate taste, 50
lessons at the rue Ballu, 58–9
neglect by the French, 1–2, 35, 131
on basic principles of music, 112–13
on conducting, 104–6, 107–8
on cross-fertilization among the arts, 131
on Dinu Lipatti, 102
on genius, 115, 117
on harmony and melodic line, 94–5
on importance of the past, 112, 116
on listening to music, 113, 114, 130
on music in France, 44, 51–2, 71–2
on music in 1947, 71–2
on musical analysis, 98–9
on musical ear, 92, 93, 94, 96
on musical roots, 43, 44, 56
on religion of music, 110
on rhythm, 103–4, 106, 114
on Schönberg, 69, 70
on synonymity of music and life, 129–30
on task of the performer, 114, 115
on virtuosi, 115
organ teacher Guilmant, 80–1
part of last flowering of French music, 35
patriotism, 52
personality, 119, 120
prejudices, general and musical, 48–9
proponent of the *grande ligne*, 52–5, 103, 105
reaction to Stravinsky's adoption of dodecaphony, 67, 68
relations with David Diamond, 124–7
relations with students, 121–2, 123, 127, 128–9, 133
selection of students, 74–5
stature as pianist, 102
sternness to uncommitted pupils, 123–4
strictness with students, 60–1
taught by Fauré, 86–90
teacher-pupil flow, 61–4
teaching routine, 122
vocal music's importance to, 99–100
weak eyesight, 10, 56, 120
wide musical knowledge, 56–7
wins Prix de Rome second prize, 7, 10
writings and opinions, 109–17
Works
La sirène, 10
La ville morte, 11

Les heures claires, 10
Rhapsodie, 10
twelve songs, 10
Boulanger, Raïssa (mother), 8, 58
Boulez, Pierre, 35, 36, 69, 85, 111–12, 126
Bowles, Paul, 73
Boyd Neel Orchestra, 107
Brahms, Johannes, 44, 51
D Major Symphony, 105
Sapphische Ode, 99
British Broadcasting Corporation, 73, 78
programme 'The Tender Tyrant', 120
Brittany, folk music of, 82
Britten, Benjamin, 16, 17, 21, 67, 113
Brocali, Gianpaolo, 66
Buxtehude, Diderik, 40

Cambridge, Mass., USA
Longy School of Music, 66
Caraman-Chimay family, 83
Carissimi, Giacomo,
Jephthah, 39
Carter, Elliott, 14
Casa Fuerte, Yvonne de, 126
Casals, Pablo, 12
Casella, Alfredo, 51, 88
Caussade, Georges, 8, 131
Cavalieri, Emilio de', 40
Cavalli, Francesco, 55
Cévennes, folk music of the, 82
Chabrier, Alexis, 88
Chagall, Marc, 77
Chanler, Theodore, 36
Chapuis, Auguste, 131
Charles, Theodore, 14
Charpentier, Marc-Antoine, 43, 76
Chatou (sur Seine), 120, 121
Chausson, Ernest, 11, 88
Chauvet, Alexis, 80
Chavchavadze, Prince George, 36, 104
Chávez, Carlos, 36
Chihara, Paul Seiko, 66
Chopin, Frédéric, 4, 11, 40, 83
Preludes, 44
Citkowitz, Israel, 36, 73
Clareus, Switzerland, 25
Claudel, Paul, 15
Protée, 29
Clefs, 101
Clermont-Tonnerre, Duchesse de, 31–2
Cocteau, Jean, 24, 29, 30, 32, 33, 38
collaboration with Stravinsky, 24
version of Sophocles' *Antigone*, 38

Index

Index

Index

Index

Index

Index

143

Index